AF333415

Days of
HEAVEN
on EARTH

Days of HEAVEN on EARTH

Steps to Intimacy with God & Your Spouse

BRENDA TAYLOR

Book design by Nancy A. Neal

The ideas expressed in this book are not necessarily those of Pathway Press.

Library of Congress Number: 93-083741

ISBN: 0-87148-2703

Printed in the United States of America

Dedication

I would like to dedicate this effort to my parents. They taught me the Word of God from infancy. More important, they have faithfully lived it.

Norman and Florene Owen are honored laypeople in their church. They have been God's chosen vessels for winning hundreds of people to Christ. Their three daughters are married to ministers. All who know Norman and Florene are challenged by their example in living for Jesus.

Thanks, Mom and Dad, for giving your lives to the Lord Jesus and to me.

Contents

Foreword

Brenda Taylor was a woman of prophetic insight. Like most prophets before her, the truth of which her words and her life bore witness gained little hearing before her death. As others have noted, prophets tend to see things at least a season ahead of the current outlook. Prophets must get accustomed to being ignored, or else they will just become hard and bitter. But anyone who knew Brenda Taylor knows that, unto the end, her heart remained as sensitive as a butterfly, her spirit as sweet as a flower. This book, now posthumously published, is a fitting tribute and witness to that sensitivity, sweetness and truth.

The pages of this book chart a path that Brenda herself traveled. It is the journey of covenant relationship with God. As I have often told my students, when the prophets set out to reveal the truth about the relationship between God and His people, most of the time they employed symbolism and terminology from two different and quite distinct arenas: the law court and family life. We tend to do most of our theology in the terms and categories of the law court. I suppose we like the clarity, precision and control of such language, and so we talk much of the things like testaments, testators, justification and pardon. Quite neglected by comparison have been the rich relational concepts and figures of family and, particularly, marital life. This is unfortunate because law court language was typically employed by the prophets when they were attempting to set forth the very *minimal terms* of relationship, especially at times of covenant breakdown. When they were ready to explore the manifold *heights* and *depths of relationship with God,* they reached for the relational analogies of parents and children, and especially of husbands and wives.

A good education can enable one to get around quite handily in a court of law, but the ability to probe and experience the deep and delicate mysteries of marital intimacy requires far more than a good education. It requires spending a good deal of time in another kind of court, namely, the court where we press into the presence of the very One who reveals and *is revealed by* the boundless wonders of marital love.

Brenda Taylor, like the prophet Isaiah, spent a good deal of time in this other court. And now, in Brenda's own words, we are blessed to be offered some choice insights from the courtship, the companionship and the consummation of that intimate relationship with her husband and her God. And those of us who know her are even more greatly blessed to have known the life that fulfilled, indeed *filled full,* these words.

Rickie Dale Moore

Preface

The impression in some religious circles is that women are almost insignificant. Yet in reading Scripture we find that God has always given us a place of prominence. Cultures have suppressed women throughout history, but where the gospel is preached, we see women blessed. Historically, Christianity has given women prominence and dignity.

The New Testament teaches that a man is the head of his marriage as Christ is the head of the Church. Men have a divine role model, but what about women? What is our position? Do we have a role model?

Good news, ladies! We *do* have a marvelous position in God's plan . . . and we have a divine role model who will constantly minister to us God's powerful plan and our exciting place in it.

Get ready for the fulfillment God planned and purchased for you. You are important to God. He wants you to know and understand that. You will be blessed as a woman, and it will not be necessary to resort to the world's ideas of womanhood to obtain the blessing. Just follow your divine role model, and it will begin to happen in your life today.

The desire for intimacy leads us to true relationships in our lives if we pursue them under our heavenly Father's guidance. Without the protection He gives, our search for intimacy can be a pursuit that exposes us to much hurt and evil.

God not only gives us the desire for intimacy, He also gives us direction in His Holy Word. His instructions are not old-fashioned and out-of-date. We can each review our own lives and see how obedience would have protected us from those terrible experiences that came from our rebellion to God's loving restraint.

I was delighted to discover that the fulfillment of my deepest need for intimacy was carefully illustrated in God's Word. He has given steps that lead us to Him. They are presented as items of furniture in the tabernacle of Moses. Each piece of furniture reveals a great truth about how we may draw near to God. They also reveal the sequence necessary for us to follow in seeking Him.

Theologians could detail any number of meanings from these symbols, I am sure. I have been blessed to see them as vital steps to intimacy with God. How special that God would give an illustration that relates so readily to us women: furniture!

As I began to take the steps and enjoy special times of intimacy with God, He began to show me another powerful truth. The same steps for intimacy in my relationship with Him were also the steps for true intimacy with my husband. I have been blessed by these truths, and now I gladly share them with you.

Brenda Taylor

Acknowledgments

To God be all glory, honor and praise! I have been the recipient of His merciful grace for many needs in my life, and I gladly share His gift of grace with others.

Special appreciation to You, Father, for blessing me with my precious husband, Al, who is my friend, lover and the delight of my life. Thank You for revealing Your love to me through him in so many wonderful ways, one of which is helping me write this book.

God, I am grateful for my godly parents who lovingly gave of their time and energy to care for me after my surgery, making it possible for me to continue writing during my convalescence.

Thank you, Father, for our daughter Fawnia, a dedicated wife and mother, who faithfully worked with me on this manuscript. Thank You for giving her strength to sacrifice weeks of her time to correct, restructure and type my handwritten manuscript.

Thank You, God, for giving Al and me a son, Todd, who has a heart for God and is willing to be open and honest. Thank You for the contribution he has made to help me see areas of my life that needed Your grace and mercy so I could change and be a better wife and mother.

Thank You, Lord, for our daughter Athena, whose love for home and family brings joy to our hearts. Thank You for inspiring her as she happily accepted and fulfilled the task of drawing pictures of the tabernacle furniture for me to have a detailed visual example for reference while writing this book.

Thank You, God, for my friend Cheryl Justice, who generously shared some of her divinely inspired poetry to be used in this book.

Thank You, Lord, for special friends, Autry and Faye Dawsey, who generously opened to us their beautiful, quiet home on the lake where we could rest and hear from God to finish our first draft.

Thank You, Father, for Kaye Stuman, who helped more than she can possibly know by patiently typing and retyping the manuscript every time we made changes.

Thank You, Lord Jesus, for the many people You raised up to intercede for Al and me during our time of writing. I cannot name them all, but one I must name: my friend Eunice Johnson, in Mora, Minnesota. Thank You for her loving labor of prayer for us every day, which has been a constant source of strength and hope, especially during the struggles.

A precious part of Brenda's legacy to us was a manuscript of her insights. The manuscript was a conveyer of a powerful message but was still in rough draft. We knew this message could bring blessing to many readers if it could be properly edited. We also know of a person who has both the gifts and the experience to do such work with true excellence.

Thank you, Nancy Neal, for being that special person who brings dreams like this into reality. Your commitment to give Christ your best is always revealed in the superb use of your talents for His glory. We are also grateful to Cari Beasley for assisting Nancy and to Hoyt Stone for his oversight and advice.

Part One

Because I have seen many women struggle with the same things I struggled with in my marriage, my heart goes out to them with compassion. Within these pages I share some of my struggles and the freedom I experienced through answers I found in God's precious Word.

God wants women to be free to be all He has created us to be. He has blessed us with womanhood that we might be a blessing. We learn our value when we put to good use all God has given us. One wonderful opportunity to do that is found in marriage.

God's plan for marriage is a marvelous one He uses to develop both man and woman. Through marriage we come to the end of ourselves to find God . . . and the realization that He is enough. He is all-in-all, the ultimate, our source, the One with whom our hearts cry out to be one.

God worked through the struggles I experienced in my marriage to conform me to the image of Christ. What a beautiful plan for God to use marriage to bring us to Himself so He can make us in His likeness!

Chapter One

God's Plan for Women in Marriage

Cocoon of Darkness

As far back as I can remember, I wanted to get married and live happily ever after. That was my idea of what life was all about, and I especially desired the "happily ever after" part. I had no idea I would have to go into a cocoon of darkness before I could see the light of happiness in marriage. But God proved Himself faithful and very personal as He answered my many questions through His Word. The Holy Spirit made His Word come alive in me as I meditated on it and put it into practice. How great God is!

My desire was to be the best wife a man could ever have. I wanted to please my husband, Al, and bless him in every conceivable way. In our courtship Al poured out his love to me in many creative ways. He made surprise visits to see me. He had a phone put in my home so he could call me. I found inspiring love notes in unexpected places. He lavished varied gifts on me, from a tailor-made suit to albums of my favorite music. He sang romantic songs to me with his deep bass voice.

He was always doing something special for my family. He took us to visit relatives and ran errands for my mother. He even took us all out to eat a meal at a restaurant (something unusual for my family in 1960). He entertained us with funny stories and shared insights from God's Word. My dad especially enjoyed discussing the Scriptures with him.

Al always seemed to find the good in people and enjoyed complimenting them. He made my whole family feel wonderful! I think all of us were in love with him.

Al took the initiative in our relationship, and I loved it! Two weeks after we met, he shocked and overwhelmed me with a proposal for marriage. I couldn't believe he was serious. He didn't know me at all but said he knew I was supposed to be his wife. Of course, I was flattered and pleased that this handsome, capable orator with the wonderful bass voice wanted to marry me. But it was all too sudden. I didn't know him. I thought, *This can't be happening to me!* It was like a dream.

Instead of responding favorably to Al's proposal, and even though I wasn't going steady, I pledged my love and loyalty to another guy I was then dating and told Al I would not date him. Before long, my boyfriend gave me his class ring. Did that hinder Al from coming to see me every day he was in town? No. Since I had not yet learned to drive, he talked me into letting him teach me. He found many ways to get into my life without taking me out for a date.

One year after he proposed, we were married. He was 22, and I was 17. We moved two hundred miles away from my parents into an upstairs furnished apartment. We had to go through the landlord's house to get to our stairway.

Reality of the "ever after" began to settle in quickly. Al was concerned about being a good provider, so he spent days and nights diligently working. His days were spent in the office as branch manager of *Encyclopedia Britannica*, and his nights were spent selling the books door to door. Most of the time he tried to come home sometime before going out to work at night. I never knew when he might show up. Each day I became increasingly lonely, especially when I became so nauseously sick and discovered I was pregnant. The hours crept slowly by, and I cried each morning as Al drove away to the office.

I loved doing things for Al and did everything I could think of for him. Besides cooking and cleaning and washing and ironing clothes, I polished his shoes, helped him dress, buttoned his shirt, put his cuff links in his sleeves—I did almost everything but tie his tie. I spoiled him because we were making the most of the little time we had together.

When it was time for our first child to be born, we realized we needed a larger place to live. We barely had room enough to squeeze the bassinet between the bed and the window. So we bought a house, had a baby and moved, all within a two-week period. During that same time, Al left to go to his great uncle's funeral a hundred miles away, which meant he would be gone all day. I wanted him to go to the funeral but felt like I needed him with me at this special time. I didn't know how to communicate my frustrations. I suppressed my anxieties and allowed fresh resentment to build along with the resentment I already felt for his being gone so many hours to work.

Al felt the pressure of providing a home for the new baby and sadness over the loss of this loved one, and I didn't understand him as I probably should have. I was busy thinking of my own needs. Unfortunately, neither of us realized how important it was to communicate our feelings to each other then, so he put it out of mind, and I continued to suppress my feelings to maintain some semblance of peace.

While Al was gone to the funeral, I was blessed to have

my mom come and help me pack so we could move when he returned. One day during her visit, Al became upset with me for turning on a burner under a new, empty glass coffee pot. I began to cry. He told me my tears were not acceptable and that he would not put up with crying from me any more. I took him seriously and tried for years to follow his instructions. Of course, I cried when he was not around if I needed to but not in his presence if I could help it. When I couldn't hold back the tears, I did my best not to let him see.

I was very insecure in this marriage. Much attention had been placed on outward appearances, and Al and I did not take time to communicate our hearts and minds to each other. The only exception was when we were so full we allowed things to spill out. Even then, those times were few and far between . . . but quite ugly.

The result was that I became more focused on trying to please Al than on being who I was. I discovered that he preferred that I be quiet, asking no questions. I thought I could handle that since I was brought up that way. I was in for a rude awakening! Inside I cried out for relationship while also I felt the need to be quiet or risk losing my husband to another woman.

I began to be jealous of the time and attention he gave other women. I was miserable, so I know I made him miserable. I tried to communicate my feelings to him, but most of the time I went about it the wrong way. The barriers between us became bigger. He let me know I was trying to limit his freedom. I did not realize I was trying to control situations to prevent the deep hurt I felt.

Our mutual commitment to God and to each other held us together while the ministry of the church, the Word and the Holy Spirit worked to change us. We discovered that many of the changes were painful . . . but wonderful. We also learned that the process is never completed in this life. However, if we had given up on each other, the spiritual growth that marriage offers would have been interrupted.

His Butterfly

One sunny morning in the early fall of 1991, I went out on the patio to have my devotions. This day I really wanted to hear from God because I was confused trying to balance my time with God, family and church. More specifically, I was troubled about whether I should travel more with my husband, Al, or stay at home.

Since Al traveled all our married life either as a salesman or in full-time stewardship ministry, I was quite active in my local church. At this time I was involved in ministry at Crowder Chapel in Cleveland, Tennessee, to reach the poor. The Holy Spirit led me to this place of love, acceptance and forgiveness where I began to pour myself as completely as I knew how into praying for, ministering to and loving the precious people of East Cleveland.

I was also trying to be a good wife to my husband. I didn't want to be preoccupied when he was home. I wanted to participate with him in his interests—traveling to share in his God-given ministry. Through some times of serious illness, though, I was beginning to realize that spiritually, physically and mentally, I wasn't up to it all.

I found myself crying out to God, "What do You want me to *do*?" As I waited to hear His answer, a butterfly lit on my knee. A butterfly landing on my knee wasn't so strange in itself, but when I moved and the butterfly remained, I thought that a bit unusual. Thinking the butterfly a distraction, I reminded myself I needed to get my mind on God so I could hear from him. I closed the devotion book on my lap. The butterfly didn't move. In fact, it seemed oblivious to any motion. I waved my hands near it, and it just sat there. Finally, I began to get the message. *Maybe God is trying to tell me something through this butterfly. . . . God, what are You trying to say to me?*

"What do You want me to *do*?" I had asked.

"Just *be* like the butterfly."

What do You mean, be like the butterfly? It's an insect; I'm a human being. How can I possibly be like the butterfly?

As I waited, I noticed the butterfly was not a rare one with unusual colors. It was just an ordinary, common-looking butterfly. I thought, *I can definitely relate!*

Then I began to reflect on what a butterfly is like and to get a picture of what God was saying. I remembered greeting cards embossed with butterflies that lifted my spirit. I thought of brightness, cheer, joy, confidence. I regarded this insect as sensitive but trusting as it remained perched on my knee. I thought of hope, faith and beauty. Finally, as I watched it fly away, I observed how light, carefree and unburdened it seemed as it sailed above all the activities on the ground. It didn't toil or spin. I thought of springtime, new life, Jesus' resurrection!

Then I remembered the butterfly hadn't always been this way. Once it was a worm. Before it could be changed, it had to experience some dark times—closed up and alone in its cocoon. But because of its struggle, it emerged from the darkness a beautiful insect, able to live a totally different life as a new creature. Now it flies *above* its circumstances instead of crawling *under* them.

God spoke to me:

Just be what I created you to be—a woman— and all that it means to be a woman. Just relax and *be*. Don't be afraid to be what you are and all you are, even if some people misunderstand. Just be like the butterfly and don't worry about what people think of you as long as you are endeavoring to be obedient to My voice. Just rest. Quit toiling and spinning, trying so hard to please. Enjoy the relationship you and I have, and I will let you know when to go, when to stay and what you should *do!* Then you will be able to bring joy, peace, cheer and life to others just by resting and letting *My* joy, *My* peace, *My* cheer and *My* life flow through you.

To be free to be like the butterfly, we as women must come out of the darkness of our struggles by allowing the light of God's Word to shine into our lives. "The entrance of thy words giveth light, it giveth understanding to the simple" (Psalm 119:130).

My prayer is that through this study God will bring light to any dark situations in your life. May you be set free to be all God has created you to be. May you experience days of heaven on earth in marital intimacy with your special man.

Our God-given Role

God never intended women to be oppressed and depressed by men or other women. He made a way for each of us to be free to communicate from *our* perspective on the issues of life.

Satan has tried for centuries to keep woman "in her place." When he is in control, he will not allow us to share from our heart things that matter. He fears the balance we bring into marriage by sharing our heartfelt insights. He has tried to belittle women because we are more emotional than men. He tries to intimidate us about communicating our feelings openly. He has succeeded in focusing great attention on outward appearance or performance, causing us to feel used. Because many women feel society does not accept them when they assume traditional roles, we have tried to think and respond more like men. This has created confusion in our homes, particularly with children. Thus, families—the very foundation of our country and the foundation of the Church— are falling apart. Sadly, this includes the Christian community, which has become increasingly influenced by the world's standards.

Women are crying for help! Some feminists have even begun to see that they have been going the wrong way. Said Sally Quinn, ". . . Many women have come to see the [feminist] movement as anti-male, anti-child, anti-family and anti-feminine. And therefore it has nothing to do with us."

Though we all need guidance, feminism is *not* the answer. The best guidance is from the One who created us, the One who loves us, the One who designed our lives—God the Father. He plainly revealed His plan for us in His Word.

Ephesians 5 says husband and wife are to reveal the mystery of Christ and the Church by their behavior toward one another. If we each understand, accept and follow our role as laid out in the Word of God, we will give our children a clearer understanding of their roles in life. Our families will be strong, our examples will draw others to Christ, and our nation will be preserved.

To live out our God-given role, we must first know what it is. To understand our role, we must follow the primary role model—God himself. To follow God and know His heart, we must become intimate with Him. Through intimacy with God we can better understand intimacy with our husbands and vice versa. Understanding more about intimacy with our husbands enables us to better fulfill our calling as women.

If we fulfill our role both in the human family and in the family of God, our children will have a definite pattern to follow. Our godly example will help them better identify who they are and be comfortable with that. They will also know what is expected of them.

Ephesians 5:22 says, "Wives, submit yourselves unto your own husbands, *as unto the Lord*" (italics added). By studying how we are to submit to the Lord, we will learn how we are to submit to our husbands.

Why?

Why dwell in the darkness
    when the light is all around?
Why stay in the shadows
    when true Sonshine does abound?
Why live like a beggar
    when He'll meet your every need?
Why die in the dungeons
    when you can be free indeed?

—Cheryl Justice

Chapter Two

Freedom Through Being Valuable

Women are different! Women are unique! Women are valuable! Women are special! Women are wonderful! God made us all that we are. And all we are in Him is *good!*

> And God said, Let us make man in our image, after our likeness. . . . So God created man in his own image, in the image of God created he him; male and female created he them. . . . And God saw every thing that he had made, and, behold, it was *very* good (Genesis 1:26-27, 31, *italics added*).

I used to wonder how and where I fit into those verses—being created in His image. I thought that if God is referred to with the masculine *He* and I'm not really like Him in shape, He must have made me like Him in the way I think, the way I conduct myself, the way I talk. I decided I must need a male image to follow because inside I must be created in the male image.

Throughout my life I became really frustrated because, try as I might, I could not think, act or talk like a man. I concluded, *I am not very valuable. As a woman I must be second class, an afterthought, a fill-in. I can never measure up to being like a man.* Therefore, I was not, in my own mind, able to meet God's expectations of me.

After talking with other women, I discovered many felt the same way. I was not alone in feeling of lesser value. I realized the solution to this problem was in gaining a greater understanding of God's words concerning women.

Divine Role Models

Since we are made in His image, let's look at woman's role through an understanding of the Godhead, beginning in Genesis.

In the account of the creation of humankind, God is referred to in the plural; that is, the Trinity: Father, Son and Holy Ghost. Genesis 1:26-27 reveals clearly that God needed both man and woman to create humankind in His image. It took two—not just man but woman also.

In the New Testament God first sent Jesus as head of the Church. Then He sent the Holy Spirit to exist within the body of the Church as an activating force.

After Jesus gave instructions, wasn't the Holy Spirit the One who set out to accomplish the work? After Jesus paid the price for our salvation, didn't the Holy Spirit come to administer it?

The role Jesus filled was absolutely necessary. The role the Holy Spirit filled was also necessary. Together they reveal completely God the Father. As I understand Scripture, the role Jesus filled revealed the mind or will of the Father. The role the Holy Spirit now fills reveals the heart or spirit of the Father.

Where do you find the mind but in the head? Ephesians 5:23 says, "For the husband is head of the wife, even as Christ is head of the church. . . ." Christ—the Head. Husband—the head. Herein lies a definite pattern for men to follow.

Where is the heart but in the body? Ephesians 5:28 says, "So ought men to love their wives as their *own bodies*. He that *loveth his wife loveth himself* "(*italics added*). This scripture indicates that the wife is the husband's body; they are one.

Trinity As Pattern for Husband and Wife Roles Under God

God	Jesus	Holy Spirit
Father	Son	Holy Spirit
God	Christ	Church
God	Head	Body
God	Husband	Wife

This parallel helps us understand the pattern God has given each of us (male and female) to follow in our roles with each other and with Him.

How valuable is Jesus? His value cannot be measured. Neither can it be increased nor diminished. However, every man's value increases as he patterns his male role after Jesus.

How valuable is the Holy Spirit? His value also cannot be measured. It can neither be increased nor diminished. But every woman's value increases greatly as she patterns her female role after the *Holy Spirit*.

Note also that the Father, Son and Holy Spirit are patterns for both men and women to follow in their spiritual walk. Here I refer to a specific and distinctive pattern or role model to enable us to identify who we are as men or women. Just knowing we have a divine pattern in the Godhead should increase our awareness of how valuable we are to God. "But I would have you know, that the head of every man is Christ; and the head of the woman is the man; and the head of Christ is God" (1 Corinthians 11:3).

The illustration on page 31 shows Christ as head of the man—with the name *Christ* above the name *Husband*. Christ is also part of God the Father because of the Trinity; they are three in one. Husband and wife are to become one flesh to reveal Jesus and the Holy Spirit working together as one. Throughout the Bible we see the Word and the Spirit functioning together to reveal the Father. The Word does not function alone but by the power of the Holy Spirit. The Word is the substance through which the Spirit works. "But the Comforter, which is the Holy Ghost, whom the Father will send in my name, he shall teach you all things, and bring all things to your remembrance, whatsoever I have said unto you" (John 14:26).

Is the Holy Spirit more valuable than Jesus? Of course not! Is Jesus of more value than the Holy Spirit? Of course not! Nevertheless, Jesus' coming to earth does precede the coming of the Holy Spirit in fullness. Yet they are not in competition with each other. One does not try to do what the other is supposed to do, but they are equal in the Godhead. One is not jealous of the other but aids the other. Each respects, honors and lifts up the other.

Adam was created first, then Eve. God did not design them to compete with each other. He didn't plan for one to try to do what the other was created to do. He created them equal but different. Jealousy was inappropriate. They completed each other. Each could appreciate the value of the other and bring fulfillment to both.

We have profound value—value placed in us by God!

When the Holy Spirit first began to help me understand that the husband is the head and the wife is the body in this "one flesh" relationship, I must admit I had to repent for not accepting myself as the *body*. When I compared the functions of the head to the body physically, I wasn't sure I liked the way God had arranged me. I wanted to do what the head does and give directions to the body. I wanted to make the decisions that affect the body and make sure those decisions were in my best interest. I thought, *Who better to make these decisions about the body than the body itself?* I really wanted to be the head *and* the body.

The body often suffers for decisions the head makes. For instance, at times the head ignores the body's need for rest to watch a TV show, play a game, attend a party or read a book. When the head decides to overeat, it ignores the body's signal it has had enough. If the head considered the body, it would not put the body through such pain without good reason. To me, the body seemed helpless, yet I realized God put me in the position of the body as a wife in a marriage relationship.

He seemed to say, "You as the body must not separate yourself from the head when the head makes a wrong decision. This does not include decisions that jeopardize life or threaten your relationship with Me. But the body should go along with the head and endure the suffering, making intercession to the One who can change him."

Wasn't this being a doormat, used and stepped on?

At the time I didn't comprehend the beauty of the union of head and body. In the physical realm, our body communicates with the head through a complex network of nerves. It is not a one-way street, head to body, but a communion of purpose marked by constant communication— head to body and body to head.

If I, the body, make a decision contrary to the head and then act on that decision, we are not in agreement. I leave the head without the support of the body, causing the head to be alone. But God said, "It is not good that the man should be alone" (Genesis 2:18). He continued, ". . . I will make him an help meet for him."

Jesus chose us to be His bride, His body (Ephesians 5:23), His wife (Revelation 19:7), and we responded to Him. In essence, my husband chose me—his bride, his wife—and I responded to him and became his body.

Jesus is the initiator, and we are responders in spiritual covenant. My husband is the initiator, and I am the responder in marriage covenant.

The Holy Spirit is a responder. "And the spirits of the prophets are subject to the prophets" (1 Corinthians 14:32).

When we join ourselves with Christ at salvation, we accept Him as He is—the Head. He left His Father in heaven (His family) and laid down all His ambitions, hopes and dreams to pay the price for us to be His bride. We respond by accepting Him as owner, subjecting ourselves to His headship. This means we have moved from dwelling alone to a position where Christ is our protector, provider and the lover of our souls. We need not try to fulfill His responsibilities in our relationship.

When I married Al, I made a commitment to accept him as he was, realizing he was also altering his plans to include me. He had to lay aside his personal, selfish ambitions, thus paying the price of laying down his life for me. He left his father and mother to live with me.

I am to accept him as head of the relationship as Jesus is head of the Church. I am to accept him as protector, provider and lover; I am not to try to fulfill these roles myself. I am to subject myself to his leadership as the Holy Spirit does to Jesus.

We know the Holy Spirit only dwells in those who have first received Jesus (see John 14:17 and Romans 8:9). The Holy Spirit works *with* Jesus. Because Jesus is there, the Spirit is there!

This is the concept of two becoming one—two distinct roles working together to form one unit. This union is essential to enjoy a life of fulfilled intimacy with our husbands. This is the foundation upon which to build the steps of intimacy.

Part Two

True intimacy in marriage cannot be attained without God. He is the source of all life. I desire to see women so united with God that their worth as a woman is no longer an issue. Submission to God's plan for marriage is one of the ways He uses to conform us to the image of Christ and bring us into unity with Himself.

Totally abandoning ourselves to God's way brings unity in our relationship with God *and* in marriage. His way is one of training and discipline. His way involves our experiencing trials, hardships, pain and suffering. If we are to really know God "in the power of his resurrection," we must know him in "the fellowship of his sufferings" (Philippians 3:10). The things we suffer teach us obedience just as Jesus' sufferings taught Him to obey. "Though he were a Son, yet learned he obedience by the things which he suffered" (Hebrews 5:8).

Many afflictions we experience come because our flesh resists God's way to go our own way. Sometimes our way feels so right but, according to God's Word, is so wrong. "There is a way which seemeth right unto a man, but the end thereof are the ways of death" (Proverbs 14:12). God's way is life revealed by Jesus, who is the Way, the Truth and the Life. He became "perfect" through His sufferings to become the "author of eternal salvation unto all them that obey him" (Hebrews 5:9). All who obey Him are called His body, the Church (see Ephesians 5:23; Colossians 1:18, 24).

The mystery of Christ and the Church is revealed to our families and to the world when both husband and wife follow Christ's example and lay down their lives for each other in the marriage relationship. Marriage is referred to in John 2:1-2 as a wedding ceremony and in Hebrews 13:4 as two individuals of the opposite sex uniting in covenant relationship. One is the beginning of this covenant; the other is the continuation of this covenant. The process that brings this marriage covenant into existence begins with *commitment* from both man and woman. The process that enables it to continue is *communion*, and the process that brings forth production is *cooperation*.

In the following chapters the tabernacle of Moses guides us through these phases. The first phase of *Commitment* is symbolized by the Outer Court. The second phase, *Communion*, is symbolized by the Holy Place. The third, *Cooperation,* is symbolized by the Most Holy Place. The Outer Court represents the *body*. The Holy Place represents the *soul (mind)*. The Most Holy Place represents the *spirit (heart)*. Jesus is the *Way* for the *body* in the Outer Court. He is the *Truth* for the *mind* in the Holy Place. He is the *Life* for the *spirit* in the Most Holy Place.

Three Jewish feasts also correspond to the three phases. The Feast of Unleavened Bread dramatizes the symbolism in the Outer Court. The Feast of Pentecost dramatizes the symbolism in the Holy Place. The Feast of Tabernacles dramatizes the symbolism in the Most Holy Place.

Before the new covenant, only the High Priest could go into the Most Holy Place to experience God's presence. Animal sacrifices were made on the brazen altar each year for those who believed in God. The person who needed forgiveness would lay his hands on the head of the animal, confess his sins and repent. Then the priest would kill the animal and sprinkle its blood on the altar. Finally, the animal was washed with water by the priest and burned with the fire on the altar according to God's detailed instructions.

This is an Old Testament picture of Jesus, the Lamb of God and the Head of the Church, laying down His life to give life to the Church. The *way* for God's people, Israel, was not yet revealed in the Old Testament. Hebrews 9:8 says, "The Holy Ghost this signifying, that the *way* into the holiest of all was not yet made manifest, while as the first tabernacle was yet standing" (*italics added*).

God has now taken away the old covenant and established the new through Jesus Christ, who is our High Priest. "Then he said, Lo, I come to do thy will, O God. He taketh away the first, that he may establish the second" (Hebrews 10:9). The first covenant was a physical pattern of spiritual things to come; that is, heart relationship with the eternal and holy God of hope. Through identifying these steps of intimacy in the new covenant (or New Testament) with the old covenant steps of intimacy taken by the priests, a definite pattern emerges for husbands and wives.

Husbands and wives must labor to enter into the rest available to us in marriage—the rest of believing in one another as we believe in Christ.

> There remaineth therefore a rest to the people of God. For he that is entered into his rest, he also hath ceased from his own works, as God from his. Let us labor therefore to enter into that rest, lest any man fall after the same example of unbelief (Hebrews 4:9-11).

That example was revealed in Hebrews 3:17-19 when the children of Israel in the wilderness were unable to enter into rest because of their unbelief. Because we believe in God, we can enjoy a love relationship of oneness that enables us to enter into the rest God has promised.

If we are to "fight the good fight of faith" (1 Timothy 6:12) to reach our goal of oneness with our husbands, we must know of our spiritual pattern set forth in God's Word. Life begins and ends with God. He is Alpha and Omega, beginning and end, the author and finisher of our faith.

My desire is to increase your awareness of Christ Jesus as He takes us through seven steps of intimacy with Himself to bring us to perfect oneness with Almighty God. I also see these steps as a pattern for intimacy with our husbands. If we submit to these steps according to the Word of God, revival will take place in our lives and spread to our families, friends and neighbors. Our value as women will increase as God's plan for womanhood is unveiled and we see the value *He* places on us. Increased confidence as wives will be ours as we understand that God's plan to use our feminine uniqueness for His kingdom begins with our husbands.

The God of the universe has chosen us to be a vital part of the body of Christ. "Ye have not chosen me, but I have chosen you" (John 15:16). We are the bride of Christ! "Let us be glad and rejoice, and give honour unto him; for the marriage of the Lamb is come, and his *wife* hath made herself ready" (Revelation 19:7, *italics added*).

Chapter Three

Commitment—Salvation

THE TABERNACLE

The Bible is filled with principles and patterns God graciously uses to communicate to us the beautiful plan He has designed for our lives. He also illustrates great truths in His plan to enable us to better grasp its complexity.

An amazing illustration of God's plan for our lives was given to us in the precise detailing of the tabernacle built by Moses. When God gave instruction to build the tabernacle, He began with the Most Holy Place. He put it first to emphasize its importance as a place of communion, fellowship, peace and rest. It is a place of knowing God as we open up to Him in honest, revealing, uninhibited communication. It is that place where we enjoy intimacy with God as we bask in His holy presence. In His presence our lives are changed and fruit is born. This is the place we long to be, for He reveals Himself to us there.

Before we reach the Most Holy Place and attain intimacy with God, however, we must take some specific steps represented by the pieces of tabernacle furniture. These steps of intimacy were taken by the priests in the tabernacle. Exodus 19 promises that we too shall be priests:

> Now therefore, if ye will obey my voice indeed, and keep my covenant, then ye shall be a peculiar treasure unto me above all people: for all the earth is mine: And ye shall be unto me a *kingdom of priests*, and an holy nation. These are the words which thou shalt speak unto the children of Israel (Exodus 19:5-6).

The New Testament confirms that the promises to Israel are available to the Gentiles because of Jesus. "That the blessing of Abraham might come on the Gentiles through Jesus Christ; that we might receive the promise of the Spirit through faith" (Galatians 3:14). Jesus Christ, the High Priest of the new covenant, "hath made us kings and priests unto God and his Father, to him be glory and dominion for ever and ever" (Revelation 1:6). This indicates that we are to function like the Old Testament priests as they approached the Holy of Holies.

As kings and priests, we can take steps toward intimacy on our way to the Holy of Holies.

These same steps parallel those steps necessary to attain true intimacy in marriage.

Seven feasts outlined in Scripture also support our understanding of intimacy with God. The feasts parallel the pieces of furniture in much of their meaning, for they were annual enactments or dramatizations of the seven vital steps to God.

We will begin now to identify those steps and feasts as they pertain to intimacy with the Father and with our husbands.

First Step of Intimacy—Brazen Altar

We begin in the Outer Court—the place of commitment. The only light here is the sun by day and the moon by night. In this area are two pieces of furniture—the brazen altar and the laver. The feasts represented here are Passover and Unleavened Bread. In the New Testament these are blended into one and called the Feast of Unleavened Bread (see Matthew 26:17).

The brazen altar, the first piece of furniture encountered, was where the priest offered a spotless lamb as a sacrifice for the sins of the people. The lamb had to be without spot or blemish to represent Christ the sinless One whose commitment as the perfect sacrifice purchased (His bride) the Church. He committed to be the Head and Savior of the Church (His body) to give her eternal life. This commitment required that He "be made flesh," leaving the comforts of His heavenly home and the love of His Father, and "dwell" among the people on earth (see John 1:1).

Christ proved His love for the Church when He fulfilled this commitment and died on Calvary. He committed that He would "sanctify and cleanse it with the washing of water by the word, that he might present it to himself a glorious church, not having spot, or wrinkle, or any such thing; but that it should be holy and without blemish" (Ephesians 5:26-27).

Through the blood of Jesus, covenant relationship is established between God and us. We commit to Him all that we are and all that we have, which is mostly sin and trouble, to receive Him and His bountiful blessings. Abundant life is available for us as we release to Him the destructive things at work in us. What joy! What relief! When we lay down the burden of sin and stop trying to manage our own lives, He forgives and takes over as Lord. He becomes the provider, protector and lover of our souls.

Commitment to Christ is made by our voluntary confession of His lordship. We believe in our hearts that He took the punishment for our sins by dying and was then victorious over that death by His resurrection. We surrender to Him to let Him fulfill His responsibilities in our lives. We accept our new role as part of the body under His headship. As the body we respond to His initiatives daily.

Similarly, in marriage women commit to our scriptural role as body under our husband's headship. We want God's best for both of us. Rebellion against our God-given roles is rebellion against Him. It also misrepresents God to the world. On the other hand, Christian marriage in scriptural order makes a powerful presentation to the world of Christ and His Church (see Ephesians 5:32).

The first step of commitment to our husbands is submission—accepting all our husbands have to give to the marriage. God ordained it. Our personal goal should be the fulfillment of our mates (see 1 Corinthians 7:3). Our mutual goal should be that we both are satisfied and complete.

Provider

In the Outer Court of the tabernacle, we find Jesus is the light who shows us the way to a life of intimacy with the Father. He is the Head and provider of the *way* for our path through spiritual life. Similarly, the husband is the head or provider for the way the wife, or the body, will go through her physical life.

Instead of our facing *spiritual* struggles and problems alone, Jesus is there. He is one with us. He will never leave us or forsake us (see Hebrews 13:5). He will lead us to abundant life in Him if we trust Him as our Good Shepherd, letting Him be head of the relationship.

Instead of our facing *physical* struggles and problems alone, our husbands are there. They are one with us. They are committed to never leaving or forsaking us but remaining with us till death parts us. They lead us to a more abundant life as we learn to trust and depend on them as head of our relationship.

Our walk with Jesus is through a covenant relationship. We covenant with Him to give Him all we are and to receive from Him all He has to give.

We covenant with our husbands to give to them all we are and to receive from them all they have to give.

The making of a covenant has a distinct and definite beginning and requires the ultimate commitment—it begins with sacrifice. Jesus' unlimited commitment was carried out on the altar of the cross. His commitment finds fulfillment when we too come to an altar of commitment, lay down our lives and take up His life as our own. He has our life, and we have His.

The Old Testament brazen altar was a symbol of this profound covenant exchange. The sacrificial lamb gave its life to atone for the sinner's debt, which could only be paid with blood. The sinner's blood was not sufficient because it would leave the sinner dead. Blood polluted by sin could not remedy the debt owed to God. The lamb was insufficient also but pointed forward to the sacrifice of Christ that would cover us once and for all.

Marriage also illustrates this truth. Relationship begins when two people willingly sacrifice to accommodate each other. As our commitment grows, so does our willingness to sacrifice for one another. Eventually we come to the place of full commitment. We meet at an altar and make the covenant of marriage, each pledging to lay down our life for the other. This kind of total commitment is the only basis strong enough for a man and a woman to build a life together. In times of trouble and stress, lesser commitments will break. But marriage is a covenant. It is permanent. It will hold until storms pass and sunshine returns to a relationship. It can hold when situations seem hopeless. It is a commitment like the one Jesus made to us.

The first step toward true intimacy is a covenant. God forbids total intimacy to any man and woman who have not bound themselves together in covenant commitment. All efforts to achieve intimacy without this commitment produce tragedy. Without commitment, each person steals from his own future and the future of his partner. They misrepresent God and His wonderful truth. Covenant commitment to each other is vital for the relationship to last.

We commit to Jesus to take His yoke upon us and learn of Him (see Matthew 11:29). Learning to receive His leadership for each step and every decision is a lifetime process. We allow His will to become our will; His dreams, our dreams. We allow Jesus to be responsible for the things He has promised to do. The Holy Spirit is Jesus' helpmeet in this. He encourages us to do as Jesus said. He supports Jesus, inspiring us to be obedient to those things Jesus has instructed.

We commit to take our husbands' yoke upon us and learn of them. Learning to receive their leadership in all things is also a lifetime process. We allow their goals to become our goals; their dreams, our dreams. We allow our husbands to fulfill their God-given responsibilities, not try to assume their roles. As women we are to be like the Holy Spirit as a helpmeet. We are to encourage our husbands in righteousness, support them and inspire them to be obedient to God.

The body of Christ doesn't decide which way to go in its spiritual walk and then ask Jesus to join its projects. The Body finds out what Christ is doing and joins His projects. Jesus is our example. He told us He did only what His Father told Him to do. "Then said Jesus unto them, When ye have lifted up the Son of man, then shall ye know that I am he, and that I do nothing of myself; but as the Father hath taught me, I speak these things" (John 8:28).

As the body of our husband, we can be one with him to such a degree that when people see us, they see our husband. Out commitment will be obvious when we follow his plans and dreams and speak those things we have heard him say. The wife does not decide which way to go in her walk with her husband and then ask him, the head, to join her. She finds out what her head is doing and joins him in completing the task.

Adam was created first (1 Timothy 2:13). Then God created Eve to join him. She was to complement what God had already planned for Adam.

Christ came to earth first, then the Holy Spirit came, completing Christ and His work (see John 15:26).

In Christ's position as head of the Church, He gives us freedom to choose and room to be spontaneous in our actions. He is patient and not hasty in His actions. He accepts the Body as we are but loves us enough not to leave us where He finds us. He is not dictatorial in His attitude. He has all the fruit of the Spirit active in His life toward us.

The pattern for men is stated clearly in God's Word. A husband's position is head of the wife, who is his body. "For the husband is head of the wife, *even as Christ* is the *head* of the church: and he is the saviour of the body" (Ephesians 5:23, *italics added*).

Women have a pattern too. Our responsibility is to submit to our husbands who have been placed as head of the relationship by God. If the body tries to be a head also, we have two heads. God says, "They two shall be one" (Ephesians 5:31). If we two are now one, there must be one head and one body. Our submission to this plan gives balance to the marriage and room to grow through good communication.

Jesus is Jehovah-Jireh—our provider. He provides food for our spirits. Jesus supplies "all . . . [our] need according to his riches in glory" (Philippians 4:19). He provides nourishment the Church needs to grow strong and increase and be lifted up in love—if we regard Him as the Head.

> And not holding the Head, from which all the body by joints and bands having nourishment ministered, and knit together, increaseth with the increase of God (Colossians 2:19).

> But speaking the truth in love, may grow up into him in all things, which is the head, even Christ: From whom the whole body fitly joined together and compacted by that which every joint supplieth, according to the effectual working in the measure of every part maketh increase of the body unto the edifying of itself in love (Ephesians 4:15-16).

> But seek ye first the kingdom of God, and his righteousness: and all these things [food, clothes, shelter] shall be added unto you (Matthew 6:33).

Wives can live according to God's principles. We can spend time learning about our husbands: how they function as men, what they like, how we can bless them. We do not need to worry about the quantity or the quality of food, clothes or shelter. As we invest ourselves in our husbands, they will increase in their ability to provide for us.

We can only enjoy the blessing of our husbands' provision for us as we submit to them as head and receive *whatever* they have to give, remembering their role is patterned after Christ. However, our obedience to God's pattern for us is not dependent on whether the husband fulfills his role.

The kingdom of God and His righteousness require us to love one another even if the person is our enemy (see Matthew 5:44). If we concentrate on doing what God requires of *us* in our relationship with our husbands, we will put the law of sowing and reaping into effect . . . and one day we will reap a harvest.

> Be not deceived; God is not mocked: for whatsoever a man soweth, that shall he also reap. For he that soweth to his flesh shall of the flesh reap corruption; but he that soweth to the Spirit shall of the Spirit reap life everlasting. And let us not be weary in well doing: for in due season we shall reap, if we faint not (Galatians 6:7-9).

If as a wife I focus on things of the flesh, I will reap a harvest of corruption. For instance, if I dwell on what *I* want instead of what Al wants, concern myself only with what I think and do not consider what Al thinks, or I meditate on what he can't or doesn't give me, I am like the person my heart may have accused him of being. But if I focus on God's image in my husband, I will reap a harvest of blessings. As I concentrate on giving him honor, respect, admiration and consideration, these graces will develop in me as they are encouraged in him (see Philippians 4:8).

Protector

Headship implies through the example of Jesus who is Jehovah-Nissi—the Lord our banner, our victor, our triumph—that we submit to our husband as protector.

Jesus is the sword of the Spirit. He is the Word, and the Word is not only provider but protector. Jesus the Word protects us from our enemies. "For the Word of God is quick, and powerful, and sharper than any twoedged sword" (Hebrews 4:12) and will reveal and cut away any destructive force in our lives. These destructive forces will eventually kill us if they are not removed.

When we submit to Christ as our protector, He begins a cleansing process in our lives that keeps the enemy from taking over. Subjecting ourselves to Him as protector causes us to become a prepared bride without spot or wrinkle.

> Husbands, love your wives, even as Christ also loved the church, and gave himself for it; that He might sanctify it and cleanse it with the washing of the water by the word, that He might present it to himself a glorious church, not having spot, or wrinkle, or any such thing; but that it should be holy and without blemish. So ought men to love their wives as their own bodies. He that loveth his wife loveth himself (Ephesians 5:25-28).

To survive spiritually, we need Jesus as our protector. When we are impatient to receive His blessings, His Word brings balance to our emotions. He protects us from spiritual pride and keeps us from being spoiled brats. We learn about trust.

In the same way, we need our husband's protection as head if we are to survive in marriage. For example, when we impatiently want a new sofa and can't afford one, our husband's reasoning ability is needed to balance our emotions. This protects us from the stress that debt causes. Stress is our enemy because it is a killer. We must learn to be more patient.

Christ is the pattern for husbands to follow as the protector. "For the husband is . . . the saviour of the body" (Ephesians 5:23). Jesus fights our battles for us. In fact, He has already defeated our enemy at Calvary. He is our protector every time we struggle with the enemy. We are victorious in Him.

Husbands like to fight our battles. They like to protect us by defending us in times of struggle. They want to protect us from intruders or anyone who would harm us. God has given them the desire to protect us from harshness and pain. If Al knows a person is harsh or crude, he makes every effort to either keep me away from that person or asks that person to modify his behavior around me. He knows I am sensitive to such behavior and doesn't want to expose me to anything that would cause me to become callous.

My husband carefully protects me from physical harm or danger. Once Al and I were visiting his dad and mom in Casper, Wyoming. As we prepared for mealtime, I arose from the dining room table to get something from the kitchen, not knowing someone had just opened a part of the kitchen floor to the cellar. Before I even realized I had stepped into this opening, Al was there pulling me out. He acted as my "protector." I appreciate what he has to offer our marriage in this area.

My husband has always been attentive to his role as provider, both in material things and things that pertain to the Word of God. As a young man, however, he was still learning about a woman's sensitivities and emotional needs.

As I shared in chapter one, when we were first married,

he was so determined to adequately provide for me that he spent most of his time working. I had difficulty with this because I rarely saw him. Therefore, we had no time for communication to help develop our relationship. I became bitter about his playing tennis or racquetball in his spare time while our relationship lacked in communion and in the development of understanding for each other. Because I missed that necessary assurance of his love, acceptance and forgiveness, my emotions were unprotected.

I did not understand the importance of taking these needs to the Father and interceding daily for my needs to be met in God's way. I also did not understand Al's perspective and did not forgive him. Receiving the provision, protection and love Al offered was difficult at first because my focus was on the things he was *not* offering. I had not talked it over with God nor had I trusted Him to work out the situations in our lives.

As a woman fashioned after the Holy Spirit and the divine sensitivity He reveals, I am also sensitive in the marriage relationship. The purpose of feminine sensitivity is to take these areas to the Father and ask *Him* to work in my husband's life *and* my own. Had I known this early on, I could have saved our marriage much heartache.

If wives (the body) receive with thanksgiving what our husbands (the head) have to give and intercede to the Father for the things they cannot give, we will be tremendously blessed with peace and joy in the Spirit. Our faith in our husbands will increase as our faith in God increases through the Word and prayer. Eventually we will see the provision and protection for which our husbands are responsible actually come into being.

Obedience to the Word not only brings the provision we desire, it also takes pressure off us as well. We will not continue to try to play God by *making* (or trying to make) our husbands conform to the Word. We will be set free from worrying about provisions because we have left them in God's hands. We will focus on God's plan for us; therefore, we will be free to fulfill His purpose in our lives.

Lover

Jesus is the lover of our souls. He loves with an everlasting love (see Jeremiah 31:3). "But God commendeth his love toward us, in that, while we were yet sinners, Christ died for us" (Romans 5:8).

> Who shall separate us from the love of Christ? shall tribulation, or distress, or persecution, or famine, or nakedness, or peril, or sword? As it is written, For thy sake we are killed all the day long; we are accounted as sheep for the slaughter. Nay, in all things we are more than conquerors through him that loved us. For I am persuaded, that neither death, nor life, nor angels, nor principalities, nor powers, nor things present, nor things to come, nor height, nor depth, nor any other creature, shall be able to separate us from the love of God, which is in Christ Jesus our Lord (Romans 8:35-39).

Let us apply this scriptural principle to our marriages. As we submit to the love our husbands have to give, trusting God to help us change and grow in mutual love, we will experience an inseparable bond of love. No matter the storms or tests that may threaten our marriage, we can stand united in God's all-powerful love, more than conquerors.

When I begin to lose my perspective of God's call for submission to my husband, I remind myself of the love my husband revealed before we were married and how easily I responded in love to him then. Though I was dating someone else when Al and I first met, Al loved me anyway. How like Christ Al was to love me while I was going in a different direction! We must remember that relationships take a lifetime of growing and that we are always moving toward a better understanding of our love for our husbands.

Can I turn that situation around and love Al even when I feel he is not showing me the love I need in a specific area? Why not receive the love he has to give in an attitude of gratefulness, trusting God to meet my needs? Why not communicate honestly with my husband and faithfully anticipate that one day he can fulfill his God-given responsibilities in a particular area?

No matter what our trials may be, we have the privilege of letting nothing separate us from the love our husbands have to give as we grow to enjoy their love to the fullest.

Jesus

If I could share with you one word;
    The greatest name you've ever heard.
If I could with one word express
    My peace and joy and happiness.
I'd have to tell you of the one
    Who lived and died and soon will come!

For my life would have no meaning without JESUS.

JESUS has given me His all.
    My mind He's changed.
    My heart He's called.
And all my life I'll not regret
The wondrous change He made in me!
    My days were dark,
    My life was sad.
What little joy I ever had
Was for a moment, I couldn't hold it,
    Without JESUS!

I know I have no peace to live . . .
    no joy to share . . .
    no love to give . . .
In fact, I haven't anything . . .
    Without JESUS!

—Cheryl Justice

Chapter Four

Commitment—Sanctification

SECOND STEP OF INTIMACY—LAVER

The second item of furniture found in the Outer Court of the tabernacle was the laver. Our English word *lavatory* is derived from the same root and carries much the same meaning, for the laver was a place of washing constructed from mirrors made from the finest brass and polished to reflect an individual.

The laver was an impressive item of tabernacle furniture. Some artists depict it as tall enough for the priest to see his reflection in its highly polished surface as he approached it. The fire and sacrifice at the brazen altar cleansed him spiritually, but the blood, smoke and ashes often left his physical appearance in need of outward cleansing. Thus, the laver was conveniently located after the brazen altar to reflect both the image of the brazen altar and the need for cleansing. We would lose hope if we saw ourselves in the laver without also seeing the brazen altar, for it is the brazen altar that reminds us of Jesus, the Word made flesh, Who made the way for us to

59

experience oneness with Him by going to Calvary.

The priest was instructed to wash his hands and feet before proceeding toward God's dwelling place lest he die (see Exodus 30:18-21). The activity at the brazen altar represents the application of Jesus' blood to destroy the power of sin over our lives. The activity of the priest at the laver represents sanctification, a deliberate act of removing from our lives anything offensive to God. It requires us to set ourselves apart from any attitude or action that could hinder or come between us and God.

As we take this step toward intimacy, we look into the mirror of the Word to see not just ourselves as we are but Christ as He is. He is the sinless One, also represented by unleavened bread in the Feast of Unleavened Bread, who is constantly available to cleanse us of any sin.

The Feast of Unleavened Bread was held the day after the Feast of Passover on the fifteenth day of the first month. For seven days the priests presented offerings made by fire, and for seven days the Israelites ate only unleavened bread. They also removed all leaven, which represents sin, from their homes. (Leaven causes bread to rise just as sin puffs up a sinner with pride and arrogance.) Its correlation with the laver represents a cleansing from sin in our lives. Under the new covenant, the blood of Jesus continually cleanses us from sin. But cleansing ourselves without the power of Calvary would be akin to washing a corpse.

In the natural, a baby begins to inhale oxygen and exhale carbon dioxide at birth. Oxygen brings life to the body, and carbon dioxide, if retained, brings death. Although blood already flows through a baby's veins, breathing imparts the precious cargo of oxygen needed by every cell. The cells receive oxygen and discharge unwanted carbon dioxide, which the blood then carries to the lungs to be exhaled. Blood also delivers nutrition needed by a newborn's cells. Concern for an infant's proper diet ensures strength and health.

Just as blood provides for growth and development and is constantly available to cleanse every cell in the body, so the blood of Jesus begins a cleansing process the day we are born into the family of God. This flow of His blood in our lives depends on our breathing in His Spirit and feeding upon the milk of His Word. His Word is reflective, like that of the laver, and reveals our constant need of cleansing. Each time we receive His Word, we receive fresh cleansing. As we hide His Word in our hearts, we come to know Him. The more we know Him, the more we love Him. The more we love Him, the more we want to please Him. If we want to please Him, then we will obey Him. Obedience will bring understanding, and increased understanding gives us confidence to share our innermost thoughts with Him, an essential part of progression toward intimacy with the Father. The entire process is an aspect of sanctification that must take place, lest we die spiritually.

As we look in the mirror of the Word and see both Christ and ourselves, we begin to identify with Him in His life, death, burial and resurrection. "Always bearing about in the body the dying of the Lord Jesus, that the life also of Jesus might be made manifest in our body" (2 Corinthians 4:10).

But to identify with Him in these four areas, we must get to know Him. In knowing Him, we learn who we are. Through the Word we can begin to see ourselves as God sees us: through the image of Christ. Deuteronomy 6:6-9 says we are to keep His words ever before our eyes. In this way, His Word becomes a part of us, and we conform to the Word—Jesus Christ. When His Word is not before our eyes, we easily lose sight of ourselves in the image of Christ, much like James referred to the priest who walked away from the laver and forgot his sinful nature and the image of the sacrifice (see James 1:24).

Identification With Christ

Identification is the alignment of oneself with another (as a person or a group) with a resulting feeling of close emotional association. According to *Webster, identify* means to be identical, to be or become the same, to establish the identity of.

Sanctify means (1) to make sacred or holy: set apart to a sacred purpose or a religious use: consecrate, hallow—"God blessed the seventh day, and sanctified it" (Genesis 2:3); (2) to make free from sin: cleanse from moral corruption and pollution: to purify. We make the decision to set ourselves apart *from* the world *to* Jesus by identifying with Him in His life, death, burial and resurrection.

Before we were born, we were in the darkness of our mother's womb. We needed deliverance from darkness to light so we could get to know our father and mother, to identify with them. The birth process was just the first step of life that brought us into light. Little by little we were exposed to things through our senses to help us know the people with whom we were to be identified. Spending time with our parents to know them and experience their love is the key to our identity. An attitude of love, acceptance and forgiveness creates the necessary environment in which a child can grow up balanced in his emotions.

God has offered us life through obedience to Him. Disobedience constitutes sin and always produces death. The provision of the laver and the Feast of the Unleavened Bread shows God's willingness to help us live victoriously over sin— not victory through denial but victory through availing ourselves of the Father's glorious provision of Jesus Christ to cleanse us by His life and His Word.

Identification With Husband

Sanctification in marriage requires setting ourselves apart from other men and from worldly desires to commit our entire life to one man. As we realize that our husband, like Christ, has changed his lifestyle to share with us, we can do the same for him. We take his name to be identified as one with him, just as Christians take Christ's name to identify themselves as one with Christ.

First we focus on how much he loves us; then we respond to his love by returning our love to him. We begin to identify with him more quickly and more strongly as we experience more of his unconditional acceptance.

As we focus on our husband's love, we learn more about him, his likes and dislikes, his habits, his strengths and weaknesses, his ways, his needs and how to meet them. We experience a growing desire to please and bless him and to truly identify with him in oneness.

We want to be seen with him. We are proud to associate with and belong to this special person. We often take on some of his mannerisms, phrases, ideas. When he feels good, we feel good. When he hurts, we hurt, because we identify with him.

We are changed simply because we separate ourselves from others and identify only with him. The endearing words he speaks to us become cleansing to our lives. In this love relationship we desire the removal of anything that would come between us.

Cleansing

Two general types of sanctification take place: (1) sanctifying ourselves and (2) allowing Christ to sanctify us. In sanctifying ourselves, we set ourselves apart from the world unto God and to hear His Word. This is dedication or consecration. In allowing Christ to sanctify us, we are cleansed through the truth, the Word of God, as we allow it to be applied to our lives.

> *Sanctify yourselves* therefore, and be ye holy: for I am the Lord your God. And ye shall keep my statutes, and do them: *I am the Lord which sanctify you* (Leviticus 20:7-8, *italics added*).

The Old Testament concentrated on outward cleansing—staying away from destructive places and refraining from destructive acts to receive more of God. "Turn not to the right hand nor to the left: remove thy foot from evil" (Proverbs 4:27).

The New Testament concentrates on inward cleansing. By feeding and meditating on the pure, unadulterated Word of God, we allow it to be assimilated in our hearts and bring about cleansing. "That he might sanctify and cleanse it with the washing of water by the word" (Ephesians 5:26).

The Word of God shows us those things that poison our hearts. It shows us the things for which we need to repent, which is a part of sanctification for the believer. "For the word of God is quick, and powerful, and sharper than any twoedged sword, piercing even to the dividing asunder of soul and spirit, and of the joints and marrow, and is a discerner of the thoughts and intents of the heart" (Hebrews 4:12).

We are encouraged to bring our sins or weaknesses to the throne room where we can talk to God about them: "Let us therefore come boldly to the throne of grace, that we may obtain mercy, and find grace to help in time of need" (Hebrews 4:16).

We discover what the Word of God has to say about our

particular need and then we follow the instructions necessary to be cleansed. "Wherewithal shall a young man cleanse his way? by taking heed thereto according to thy word" (Psalm 119:9).

On a daily basis we must continue to put the Word in our minds so it may dwell in our hearts. We must meditate on it for power over sin. "Thy word have I hid in mine heart, that I might not sin against thee" (Psalm 119:11).

Meditation

Meditating on the Word of God is rare in the lives of Christians who try to maintain hectic schedules. Yet great value is found by all who obey this oft-repeated command of God.

God illustrated the importance of meditation through the strict dietary laws of the Jews. He commanded that they eat only the clean animals He specified and not the unclean beasts. He told them how to differentiate between the beasts. "Whatsoever parteth the hoof, and is clovenfooted, and cheweth the cud, among the beasts, that shall ye eat" (Leviticus 11:3).

He went on to name both the clean and the unclean so there would be no confusion. If you study the animals, you will see that none of the clean animals eat blood, flesh or dung, so their bodies don't have the added stress of trying to eliminate those poisons. From the beginning they are cleaner because they do not take pollution into their bodies. Without understanding why, clean beasts separate themselves from certain impurities. We too should separate ourselves from certain evils God has specified as we partake of the pure Word of God—neither adding nor taking anything away (see Deuteronomy 4:2; Proverbs 30:5-6; Revelation 22:18-19).

Acceptable beasts are cleaner also because they ruminate (chew the cud). They regurgitate their food and chew it again up to three times before it goes into their intestines. The result is that they enjoy better digestion than unclean beasts. Their food is so well broken down that nutrients are dispersed throughout the body of the beast, bringing health to all parts of its body and leaving only the waste to be eliminated.

Like Jeremiah, we can find God's words and eat them. As the Holy Spirit quickens them to our hearts through meditation, they will become the "joy and rejoicing" of our hearts and bring health to our spirits and bodies (see Jeremiah 15:16 and Proverbs 4:20-22).

Animals with cloven hooves are also cleaner because they perspire through their hooves, eliminating the naturally occurring toxins that would otherwise remain in their systems.

We are further cleansed in our spiritual walk after meditation when we accept the ministry of the Word to reveal the thoughts and intents of our hearts (see Hebrews 4:12). The Holy Spirit will then lead us to confess spiritual impurities in our lives, which makes our cleansing complete.

We can easily see why God used beasts that both chew the cud and have cloven hooves to illustrate spiritual cleanliness. Animals that chew the cud bring back to their mouth for further processing that which would otherwise be indigestible. The believers' confession of sin brings back to the mouth things in our lives that must be resolved but can only be resolved through confession. We cooperate with the Word and the Spirit when we obediently confess our iniquities, removing them completely from our lives as God changes our hearts and does that work in us we can never do by our efforts.

This should also help us realize we cannot take the Word and use it as a set of rules. Through meditation we allow the Word to get into our hearts where the Holy Spirit can do His work of quickening and cleansing. We can so focus on God and His Word that we never become like the Pharisees, who had no spiritual life in them. We can be so filled with the Word that we reflect Jesus' life to others. "Who also hath made us able ministers of the new testament; not of the letter, but of the spirit: for the letter killeth, but the spirit giveth life" (2 Corinthians 3:6).

We can be wives who focus on the good in our husbands and what they have to offer us in marriage. We will find ourselves becoming less selfish and more giving as we consciously separate ourselves from everything that would hinder our relationship.

God has made women capable of giving much love, devotion and affection. As we make our husbands the only object of our love (with God first), then we can follow our husband wherever God leads him. We can endure hardships with him and enjoy pleasing him alone. We can enjoy a union so close that it brings about separation from anything that would come between the two of us.

Identity in the Marriage Relationship

If we are to serve God and our husbands, we must be secure in the knowledge of who we are. We must know where we came from and where we are going. We must understand that all we have was given to us by God.

Jesus knew ". . . that the Father had given all things into his hands, and that he was come from God, and went to God" (John 13:3). It was important for Jesus to know His identity before He could effectively minister to His disciples and others. Surely it is important for us as women to know who we are in order to minister to our husbands.

"He [Jesus] riseth from supper, and laid aside his garments; and took a towel, and girded himself. After that he poureth water into a basin, and began to wash the disciples' feet, and to wipe them with the towel wherewith he was girded"

(John 13:4-5). Jesus was confident in His knowledge of who He was and who He represented. He was therefore able to stand naked before those who were close to Him. He was so secure He could put on the apparel of a servant and humble Himself to serve His disciples. These disciples represent those whom Jesus prayed would be one with Him just as He and His Father are one (see John 17:11). He was one with them, yet served them.

Made in His Image

We have already discussed that we are made in God's image and that it takes a male and a female to properly reveal the image of God. But how are we made?

> And the Lord God caused a deep sleep to fall upon Adam, and he slept: and he took one of his ribs, and closed up the flesh instead thereof; and the rib, which the Lord God had taken from man, *made* he a woman, and brought her unto the man (Genesis 2:21-22, *italics added*).

The word *made* is from the Hebrew word *panah*, which means builded, skillfully formed.

"And Adam said, This is now bone of my bones, and flesh of my flesh: she shall be called *Woman*, because she was taken out of Man" (Genesis 2:23, *italics added*). The Hebrew word for *woman* in this verse is *Ish shah*, which is the feminine of *Ish* (meaning "of man"). It means female-man, she-man, womb-man, man with the womb.

How special! We are woman—the man with the womb (womb-man). We carry and birth the fruit of this husband-wife union. We are responsible for bringing forth the lives of our precious children into this relationship. Again, we see that we are patterned after the Holy Spirit, the agent of the new birth.

> Jesus answered, Verily, verily, I say unto thee, Except a man be born of water and of the Spirit, he cannot enter into the kingdom of God. That which is born of the flesh is flesh, and that which is born of the Spirit is spirit. Marvel not that I said unto thee, Ye must be born again (John 3:5-7).

Something Feminine About God?

God promised Abram that He would make of him a great nation (Genesis 12:2), making his seed as the dust of the earth (Genesis 13:16) and as the stars in the heavens (Genesis 15:5). As time passed and Sarai bore no children, Sarai and Abram agreed to an alternate plan—that Abram's seed come from Hagar, Sarai's maid. So Ishmael was born. But God wanted his nation to be birthed by Abram's own flesh. Abram and Sarai were husband and wife—"one flesh."

When God made the covenant with Abram, He made it with Sarai also because the two were one. He changed not only Abram's name to Abraham but Sarai's name to Sarah, representing His covenant with them both. "And I will bless her, and give thee a son also of her: yea, I will bless her, and she shall be a mother of nations; kings of people shall be of her" (Genesis 17:16).

In Genesis 17:1 the Lord appeared to 99-year-old Abram, saying, "I am the Almighty God; walk before me, and be thou perfect." "Almighty God" is translated *El Shaddai* in the Hebrew. *El* means "Strong One" and *Shaddai* means "Breasted One." According to *Dake's Annotated Reference Bible*, this pictures God as the all-bountiful One, strong nourisher, strength-giver, satisfier, supplier of the needs of His people.

God reassured Abram that He is the Fruitful One and

the Strong-Breasted One who would bring forth life (strength-giver). Twenty-four years from the time God first told him he would become a nation, Abram needed encouragement from God. God did not mind referring to Himself in the feminine. In fact, He chose this way to reveal part of His character.

> As an eagle stirreth up *her* nest, fluttereth over *her* young, spreadeth abroad *her* wings, taketh them, beareth them on *her* wings: *So the Lord* alone did lead him, and there was no strange god with him (Deuteronomy 32:11-12, *italics added*).

God doesn't apologize for being compared to a mother eagle. He is not uncomfortable with bearing attributes that we perceive to be feminine. This simply reveals more of His nature from which we were fashioned.

"For thus saith the Lord. . . . As one whom his mother comforteth, so will I comfort you; and ye shall be comforted in Jerusalem" (Isaiah 66:12-13). Here God reveals Himself comforting like a mother.

"O Jerusalem, Jerusalem, thou that killest the prophets, and stonest them which are sent unto thee, how often would I have gathered thy children together, even as a hen gathereth her chickens under her wings, and ye would not!" (Matthew 23:37). What a precious picture Jesus gives us here! Such tenderness in the heart of the Lord!

And women are like God, for we are made in His image!

Weaker Vessel—What Does That Mean?

"Likewise, ye husbands, dwell with them according to knowledge, giving honour unto the wife, as unto the *weaker vessel*, and as being heirs together of the grace of life; that your prayers be not hindered" (1 Peter 3:7, *italics added*).

"Weaker vessel" always sounded demeaning to me until I understood what it really meant.

"Weaker vessel" means a more delicate vessel than the man, who is made like a tough piece of pottery that can withstand the pressures of life. A woman is like a beautiful, fragile vase, easily broken and sensitive.

Who is the most sensitive of the Godhead but the Holy Spirit? "And whosoever speaketh a word against the Son of man, it shall be forgiven him: but whosoever speaketh against the *Holy Ghost*, it shall not be forgiven him, neither in this world, neither in the world to come" (Matthew 12:32, *italics added*). Of course, this neither equates the Holy Spirit with women nor does it equate the importance of the Holy Spirit with the importance of women. It's merely a parallel.

However, in the case of husband and wife, it appears that God *does* consider a man dishonoring his wife a serious offense. Peter said that without consideration for his wife, a man's prayers will be hindered (see 1 Peter 3:7). But God will forgive him of this offense if he asks with a repentant heart.

Women are more sensitive, and our hearts break more easily than a man's. The man is the head, and the mind is located in the head. The woman is the body, and the heart is located in the body. The mind is more reasonable, whereas the heart is more emotional.

We need the reasoning the head offers, just as he needs the emotional responses we have to offer *(i.e.*, our sensitivities). Of course, when our sensitivities are positive, the husband is usually pleased. Likewise, we all are pleased when the Holy Spirit's responses to us are positive. When we sense things that are not good in our home, in our husband's life or in the way he treats us, our husband may attribute our sensitivities to our being too emotional, having PMS or some other "female" problem. As Christians we may remember treating the Holy Spirit in a similar fashion. When there is something not good in our lives and the Holy Spirit makes us feel uneasy, we many times attribute our sensitivity to other things. We often do not value what the Holy Spirit senses and says as He communicates to us so we may benefit and grow.

For instance, as we try to encourage someone, we may gradually detect a growing tension between us. We might attribute the tense feeling to the other person's bad attitude or perhaps to one or the other of us not feeling well. Later, the Holy Spirit begins to show us we ourselves were responding in condemnation or judgment toward that person rather than truly giving encouragement. As a result, he or she was no longer able to receive what was being said.

The Holy Spirit is so gentle it is easy to ignore Him. He will not force us to listen, though He will search for ways to continue speaking to us until we either receive or totally reject His message.

Note that *Holy Spirit* (*rucha*) is found in the feminine gender in Aramaic, which is probably the language Jesus spoke when He was on earth. Holy Spirit is in the neuter in the Greek (*pneuma*), the language from which the New Testament was translated. Other languages present the *Holy Spirit* in the feminine gender as well.

Though I am in no way saying the Holy Spirit is female, I *do* believe with all my heart that the Holy Spirit is a definite pattern for women. If both sexes look at the similarities of women and the Holy Spirit, we will be better enlightened as to how to deal with women. Women can more easily accept themselves once they realize these characteristics they thought unattractive can be disciplined by the Word to become their greatest assets.

The sooner we accept ourselves, the sooner others will be able to accept us. The more aware we become of our value as women, the more readily others can respect us as women.

We can become so focused on being a devoted wife to our husband that other distractions will lose their importance. Thus, we can take another step of intimacy with our husband and cause him to feel more valuable. We set ourselves apart—sanctify ourselves, so to speak—within the marriage, and this is holy service unto God.

Let us surrender our hearts to the commitment we have made to become one with this special man. Let us allow our devotion to be to him and to no other man.

We must not be afraid to look into the laver and see ourselves as we really are. However, let us be sure that as we look into the laver, we see Jesus there too and realize we can do all things through Christ who strengthens us (see Philippians 4:13). We can do nothing in our own selves.

Women must also realize we can carry our sensitivities too far and actually overwhelm our husbands. We should be honest about our tendencies to talk too much, sometimes saying the wrong things at the wrong times. Face the fact that we give in to the temptation to be impatient with our husbands when they don't do those things we think they know to do. Let us realize that we sometimes forge ahead and try to work things out without consulting them. We don't always try to stay in unity.

Remember, God accepts each of us right where we are, but He also loves us enough not to leave us there. God is never looking for a reason to abandon us. Yet He knows, and we know, that there are many changes yet due in us. So He is always working to bring those necessary changes. The good news then declares that we are already accepted in the Beloved, and as we yield, He is making changes in us that conform us to heaven's patterns.

A Garden in My Heart

There's a garden in a valley
  where sweet dreams are ne'er forgot.
There's a stream of lifelong pleasures
  flowing through.
All the spring-fed flowers blooming
  bring forth fragrances of love.
And I'll hide it, Love, from everyone but you!

There's a loveseat made of marble
  carved by tenderest of touches.
There it's set beneath the mountain's
  perfect hue.
All the birds are ever singing sweet
  new melodies of love.
I'll not share it, Love, with anyone but you!

This, the Garden of Contentment in
  the Valley of Delight
Is the home of fondest feelings
  all for you.
Now I'll tell you where it is, Love,
  for you'll always find it near.
It's in my heart, Dear, and for no one but
  you!

—*Cheryl Justice*

Chapter Five

Cooperation—Stewardship

Third Step of Intimacy—Table of Shewbread

Laying Down Our Lives

God has another object lesson for us in the tabernacle. The next piece of furniture is found in the Holy Place behind the first veil. On the table of shewbread is the broken unleavened bread, which corresponds with the Feast of Firstfruits. It represents the laying down of the first and best of everything. It acknowledges the lordship of Jesus Christ. He is Creator and Redeemer. He is owner and provider. He is the only begotten Son of the Father who laid down His life for us and became the firstfruits—the first of many sons and daughters of the Father.

Both the table of shewbread and the Feast of Firstfruits deal with stewardship. What do we do with all God has entrusted to us? How do we manage it? "Speak unto the children of Israel, and say unto them, When ye be come into the land which I give unto you, and shall reap the harvest thereof, then ye *shall bring a sheaf of the firstfruits of your harvest* unto the priest" (Leviticus 23:10, *italics added*).

And the meat-offering thereof shall be two tenth deals of fine flour mingled with oil, an *offering* made by fire unto the Lord for a sweet savour: and the drink-offering thereof shall be of wine, the fourth part of an hin. And *ye shall eat neither* bread, *nor* parched corn, *nor* green ears, *until* the self-same day that *ye have brought an offering unto your God*: it shall be a statute for ever throughout your generations in all dwellings (Leviticus 23:13-14, *italics added*).

"The *first of the firstfruits* of thy land thou shalt bring into the house of the Lord thy God" (Exodus 23:19, *italics added*). *Vine's Expository Dictionary of Biblical Words* defines firstfruits as "the principal part or the chief part of the earliest ripe of the crop or the tree."

Once we have taken the second step toward intimacy with God, sanctification or setting ourselves apart unto only God, we are ready to begin serving Him by giving Him the best of the first in our lives (see Matthew 6:33).

This requires laying down our lives. "Then said Jesus unto his disciples, If any man will come after me, let him deny himself, and take up his cross, and follow me" (Matthew 16:24). To lay down our lives, we must *first receive life*. Again, this life comes from God's Word, the Bread of Life, which reveals His love, acceptance and forgiveness of us. As we know Him through His Word, the Bread, we trust Him. We see Him as a God of truth and faithfulness, a rewarder of those who diligently seek Him. He is the God of the universe who has all things and freely gives all things to those who love Him.

Our love for Him is revealed by our freely giving all. Our all is so meager compared to His and is, frankly, not much for

Him to ask. Isn't it great that He only requires the firstfruits as a way of saying we have surrendered all?

As we receive the life of God into our lives, we have life to give to our husbands. As we receive our husband's love, in whatever way he can give it, we can respond in an attitude of submission.

Submission to God allows Him to do His part in fulfilling His responsibilities. By not trying to assume His role, we can submit to Him and accept ourselves as the body of Christ, which is dependent on the head. Christ—*the Head*—needs the Church—*the body*—to have an attitude of submission if His will and work are to be accomplished through us and if we are to see His kingdom and righteousness established.

Our husband's greatest need in marriage is to be submitted to by his wife. A woman's greatest need is to be loved by her husband. This is a cherishing love, *agape* love, which does not expect anything in return.

Husbands are commanded over and again to love (*agape*) their wives. And women are told over and again to submit to (to be in subjection, to obey) their husbands.

Adam revealed man's tendency not to love (agape) his wife in the garden. When Eve partook of the fruit from the tree of knowledge of good and evil, Adam stood "with her." His God-given responsibility was to love, provide for and protect her. He knew what God had said about that tree, yet he did not protect his wife.

> And when the woman saw that the tree was good for food, and that it was pleasant to the eyes, and a tree to be desired to make one wise, she took of the fruit thereof, and did eat, and gave also unto her husband *with her*; and he did eat (Genesis 3:6, *italics added*).

The New Testament never mentions Eve as bearing the responsibility, only Adam. "Wherefore, as by one man sin entered into the world, and death by sin; and so death passed upon all men, for that all have sinned" (Romans 5:12). To love her without expecting anything in return, Adam could have refused to eat the fruit she gave to him. He could have protected her and thus would have been "the saviour of the body" (Ephesians 5:23). "For the unbelieving husband is sanctified by the wife, and the unbelieving wife is sanctified by the husband" (1 Corinthians 7:14).

Eros and *Agape*

Husbands have fewer problems expressing an aggressive *eros*, or erotic love (of, devoted to or tending to arouse sexual love or desire). However, to love a wife when she is unlovable, to be aggressive in charitable love (*agape*), is a challenge. God commands the husband to charitably love his wife, to cherish her and lay down his life for her.

Some wives cry out for *agape* love in their marriages. They feel used and abused by their own husbands. They want intimacy in a lasting way with a communion of hearts—the ability to express their innermost feelings and hear from their husbands the same way. Many women are ignored by their husbands when they share their opinions or express how they *feel* about a matter. Sometimes they are told by their husbands they don't know what they are talking about. Still, wives long to be heard and considered in their emotions and weaknesses.

Submission/Subjection

Subjection is defined *hupotasso* (*hupo*—"under"; *tass*— "to arrange"), to put in subjection. The body (wife) is located *under* the head (husband). *Submit* is defined *hupeiko* (*hupo*— "under"; *eiko*—"to yield"), to yield, submit. This does not mean men are never to yield but that we women need yielding emphasized in our role.

Since subjection means "under," and the wife (the body) is to submit to her husband (the head over the body), could it be that our consciousness of being "under" causes us to fear that our feelings are not being considered and that we are not thought valuable? Often we set out to prove we are valuable by taking situations into our own hands to show our husbands we are perfectly capable. Our real desire is that our husbands appreciate what we have to offer the marriage, even if the contribution seems negative to them.

One of the ways a man can obey the scriptural mandate to lay down his life is to deliberately consider valuable what his wife has to contribute. She may be more emotional and may sound unreasonable to him, but she will begin to feel loved through such consideration. She can then more easily respond in loving ways to her husband. This does not mean he will do everything she suggests or act on her every whim. But he will honor her by respecting and weighing carefully those things she senses need consideration before a decision is made.

Getting His Attention

Because we want our husband's attention, a woman sometimes encourages lust from him. When we *concentrate* on decorating or accentuating the outward form more than the inner person of the heart, we will never be satisfied with the attention we receive. Insecurity and/or rebellion will begin to take hold in our lives.

Look at women who have experienced this in the extreme. Marilyn Monroe and Jayne Mansfield, sex symbols of the past, were unhappy women whose lives came to tragic, early endings. They were appreciated for their outward appearance and their performance but were considered flighty and flippant. Their emotions were considered valuable only in the context of their sensuality.

Although their actions called for men to idolize them, both were sensitive and needed to be loved for who they were inside. Perhaps they were in rebellion to men (trying to control the men before the men could control them). They may have been trapped by insecurity (*i.e.,* not feeling loved for who they were). Whatever the cause, they fell prey to the wrong kind of attention. Lust and idolatry were at work.

"For rebellion is as the sin of witchcraft, and stubbornness is as iniquity and idolatry. Because thou hast rejected the word of the Lord, he hath also rejected thee . . . " (1 Samuel 15:23).

When more emphasis is placed on the physical than on developing the relationship through communication of hearts, lust is most likely at work. This puts any marriage in a precarious situation. Lust (covetousness) and idolatry usually go hand in hand.

> For this ye know, that no whoremonger, nor unclean person, nor *covetous man, who is an idolater,* hath any inheritance in the kingdom of Christ and of God (Ephesians 5:5, *italics added*).

> Mortify therefore your members which are upon the earth; fornication, uncleanness, inordinate affection, evil concupiscence, and *covetousness, which is idolatry* (Colossians 3:5, *italics added*).

Aggression or Rebellion

When we reject the Word of the Lord in our conversation or manner of living, we are in rebellion. When we decide to step in and do what our husbands are called to do (because we think we know more or think we can do it better than they), we are going our own way. We are stubbornly saying, "This man is incapable of carrying out his responsibilities; God doesn't know what He is talking about when He tells me to submit to this man." Remember God, not man, put these responsibilities on the husband as the head. God will help him learn the things he needs to learn if we allow God to direct our steps and wait patiently, keeping in mind the goal—though it may take years.

Our husbands can do whatever God requires of them if we give to them the same consideration we expect from them. Here is where we can lay down our lives for our husbands. We become willing for our husbands to be the head of this union. We give up trying to be the head and enjoy being the body. We give the first and the best we have to give. We become good stewards of all we are and all we have. We begin to learn the mystery of Christ and the church: "My life for yours." Jesus became the broken bread and the poured-out wine for us. If we are to be like Jesus, we can do no less for others . . . starting with our husbands.

The Holy Spirit's marvelous sensitivities are not just to be acclaimed and embraced when the spiritual gifts are in operation. Our love and acceptance of the Holy Spirit should not be based on His mighty gifts or exciting performances of His power. We should embrace Him for who He is and honor Him whether He is blessing or convicting. Wives need recognition and love from their husbands whether they are blessing him or communicating their needs to him.

Many women long to have their husbands hold them for no obvious reason except that they cherish them and are there for them. A woman needs to know her husband is there for her emotionally and spiritually as well as physically.

Remember woman's greatest need is to be loved for who she is in her innermost being. Man's greatest need is to be submitted to by his wife. Eve revealed the tendencies of woman's old nature. She acted aggressively without consulting God or her husband. In a sense, she separated herself from both and became independent by taking the forbidden action of eating the fruit. She could not be one with her husband in this action because she did not talk with him and reach an agreement before she acted. Their unity was lost, their oneness crippled.

Women *do* have an aggressive nature, which when directed by the Word of God is a wonderful thing. But going ahead and doing what we think "needs to be done" without the consent of the husband is not the time or setting in which to exercise that aggression. Neither are we to take over our husband's lack of fulfilling his responsibilities. Our goal should be to lift him up in his weak areas, to encourage him to do those things for which he is responsible. This will make him a better man, one who is more capable than if we do for him what he is supposed to do.

We understand this principle in the physical realm. For example, let's say my husband loses the use of his legs and the only way for him to be restored is for him to exert his own energy to strengthen his muscles. Suppose I don't want him to go through the pain of doing it himself. I might say, "I am more capable. I am not weak in that area, so I will pick up your legs and move them for you." If I never encourage him to fulfill his own responsibility to expend his own energy and to go through the time and pain required to eventually walk on his own, then I condemn him to the life of a cripple. His only hope would be to overrule my sympathy and aggressively take the painful but necessary steps to be strong again.

Many wives encourage their husbands to be cripples by not allowing them the opportunity to suffer to learn to be responsible in the areas God has called them—provider, protector, lover.

This aggressiveness is why God emphasizes submission on our part. Our aggressive nature is for at least two particular areas of life. One is our children. God has given us a sense of how to take care of them and make decisions about them daily while our husband is away.

The other area is prayer. We are patterned after the Holy Spirit. We too are communicators. We have the privilege of taking everything to God in prayer. Every problem we perceive in ourselves, our husbands, our children or anyone else, we can take to the Father. Instead of gossiping, we can tell God. Instead of communicating accusation, condemnation or judgment to our husband, we can express our innermost feelings to our Father in Jesus' name. We can pour out our hearts to Him and intercede for those in need.

This is a powerful way to use our aggression. I believe God has created us for this purpose. Women like to talk and have much to communicate because we are the "body." We receive many things that need a response. What better opportunity for fulfillment without hurting anyone than to take a situation to Jesus! Here we have the opportunity to be *aggressive* by praying to Him, and yet we can be *submissive* by surrendering everything. As we give Him all we are, He begins to work in our lives and in the lives of our loved ones. Instead of our trying to take care of all the problems and weaknesses we see, we can leave them in God's hands. What a fantastic plan! How relieved we can be that God made us aggressive in such a way that we can be fulfilled as a woman and come to a place of rest at the same time!

Laying Down My Life

If we are to know Christ in the power of His resurrection

as the body of Christ, we must suffer and die with Him. "That I may know him, and the power of his resurrection, and the fellowship of his sufferings, being made conformable unto his death" (Philippians 3:10). If I want to know my husband and see him resurrected, I must as his body figuratively be willing to suffer and die with him.

Didn't Jesus' death-to-bring-us-life reveal that the greatest fulfillment in life is to see someone else born into life through our own suffering? "Greater love hath no man than this, that a man lay down his life for his friends. Ye are my friends, if ye do whatsoever I command you" (John 15:13-14).

Do we have this kind of love for our husbands? We certainly must not expect them to lay down their lives for us if we are not willing to lay down our lives for them. Of course, we can only do this through Christ who strengthens us.

> Likewise, ye wives, be in subjection to your own husbands; that, if any obey not the word, they also may without the word be won by the conversation of the wives; while they behold your chaste conversation coupled with fear (1 Peter 3:1-2).

To what does the "likewise" in verse 1 refer? Chapter 2 of 1 Peter gives us an example of the kind of submission God expects from us (vv. 13-17). An act of submission to God first prepares us to obey His Word no matter what He tells us to do. Then we are ready to submit to man as God directs.

In 1 Peter 2:19-20 is another example that involves submission to someone who is not good and gentle but contrary and stubborn:

> For this is thankworthy, if a man for *conscience toward God* endure grief, suffering wrongfully. For

what glory is it, if, when ye be buffeted for your faults, ye shall take it patiently? but if, when ye do well, and suffer for it, ye take it patiently, this is acceptable with God (1 Peter 2:19-20, *italics added*).

Following is yet another example of Peter's use of the term *likewise*. He uses the term to connect a body of information and help us to focus the meaning upon our own situation. Observe:

> For even hereunto were ye called: because Christ also suffered for us, leaving us an example, that ye should follow his steps: Who did no sin, neither was guile found in his mouth: Who, when he was reviled, reviled not again; when he suffered, he threatened not; but committed himself to him that judgeth righteously: Who his own self bare our sins in his own body on the tree, that we, being dead to sins, should live unto righteousness: by whose stripes ye were healed. For ye were as sheep going astray; but are now returned unto the Shepherd and Bishop of your souls (1 Peter 2:21-25).

Following this message about Christ, he makes the connection with "likewise" in 1 Peter 3:1. Of course, Jesus is the supreme example for both men *and* women. But in these verses, women are specifically addressed.

Romans 5:8 declares that while we were yet sinners, Christ died for us. Are we willing to "die" to self for our husbands and others in our lives that they may be born into new life because they see Jesus in us? As we transfer the "likewise" from the Scriptures and make it a part of our heart and mind, we incorporate Christlike qualities into our lives. The resulting change in our husbands is the consequence of his living with the Christ in us.

If our husband is a Christian but does not obey the Word in a particular area, are we willing to die to ourselves that he may eventually see the error of his way and be changed by Jesus? If "yes," then we are following Christ's example to lay down our lives. All the changes that have come into our lives for good are the result of Christ laying down His life for us. As we follow His example, we become like Him and enable the Holy Spirit to bring good changes in the lives of our mates and children.

Jesus said, "If any man will come after me, let him deny himself, and take up his cross, and follow me. For whosoever will save his life shall lose it: and whosoever will lose his life for my sake shall find it" (Matthew 16:24-25).

Wives are told in Ephesians 5:24, ". . . As the church is subject unto Christ, so let the wives be to their own husbands in every thing."

Yes, this is a heavy message, but the consequences are also heavy. 0As we heed this admonition, husbands are helped to receive eternal life. If we disregard the message, husbands will be deprived of one of the powerful avenues and a great opportunity for God's grace to reach them.

The laying down of our lives for our husbands is similar to what women experience when giving birth. For some nine months we carry a baby while our body provides sustenance for the child. We change our diets to make sure our baby receives sufficient nutrients to grow healthy and strong. Our sleeping habits change because we have to make allowances for this baby when we lie down. We become larger and sensitive around the middle and have to buy larger, loose-fitting clothing.

Any physical or emotional weaknesses we have usually show up some time during these nine months. As each weakness shows up, we are motivated to change anything that may not be healthy both to feel better personally and to help the baby have every chance of being healthy.

When the time comes for the baby's birth, more changes occur. The body goes through much pain and travail to bring this child out of darkness into light. When the travail is over, we soon forget the anguish because of the joy we experience over the child's birth.

Wives may also have to make many life changes for the men we love. We can be sure some problems and sins will show up in our own lives as we wait for our husbands to change in a particular area. This gives us an opportunity to let God change us too.

If we want our husbands to be the best they can possibly be, we must be willing to lay down our lives for them. When they are changed to new life in needed areas, we soon forget the pain and suffering that preceded the change. We rejoice that a man is born.

Jesus said, "A woman when she is in travail hath sorrow, because her hour is come: but as soon as she is delivered of the child, she remembereth no more the anguish, for joy that a man is born into the world" (John 16:21).

We are to obey our husbands in all things, according to Scripture, unless they tell us to do something contrary to the Word of God. Only when told to do something that would jeopardize our salvation are we to appeal to a higher authority (Jesus Christ) and obey God rather than man.

There will be some suffering and some misunderstanding in our relationships, but "it is better, if the will of God be so, that ye suffer for well doing, than for evil doing. For Christ also hath once suffered for sins, the just for the unjust, that he might bring us to God, being put to death in the flesh, but quickened by the Spirit" (1 Peter 3:17-18).

When we deny ourselves and take up the cross of Christ,

we will follow Him and do "likewise," which means suffering for wrong decisions the head makes. In one sense, "the just" may refer to the wife in this particular area if she is walking in obedience. "The unjust" may refer to the husband if he is not obeying the Word in that same area.

Look what happens as a result. We are quickened, made alive in Christ! We learn during this time of suffering to put our dependence on our husband into the hands of God, especially since our ultimate dependence is always on God himself. We learn to trust God for things we cannot see, walking by faith and not by sight (see 2 Corinthians 5:7) We learn to allow our conversation (behavior, lifestyle) to be chaste—conformed to the image of Christ. "While they (husbands) behold your *chaste conversation* coupled with *fear*" (1 Peter 3:2, *italics added*).

Chaste means pure from carnality, modest (*Vine's Expository Dictionary of Biblical Words*). *Pure* means free from moral fault or guilt. *Modesty* stresses avoidance of anything brazen, bold, wanton or suggestive in behavior, speech or appearance. *Conversation* means manner of living, conduct or behavior, sexual intercourse, oral exchange of sentiments, observations, opinions, ideas. Our conduct should be such that our actions reveal that we trust God to change us (wives) first.

Scripture supports the notion that women have a powerful affect on their husbands and can win them over to the Word of God by our Christlike behavior, speech and appearance (see 1 Peter 3:1-2). What a promise! We can follow Christ's example and reap a harvest in our husband's life that will affect us (the body) in an extraordinarily positive way!

We can speak and live in agreement with God's Word and believe God to do the changing. We can release our husbands to the Father and quit trying to make these changes happen. We are free to be chaste and let God do His work, never giving up on our husbands.

Does God give up on anyone? No!

Is God long-suffering? Forgiving? Is He full of love and joy toward everyone? Or does He just love "believing" women in this special way? Does He accept us where we are but love us enough not to leave us there? Is He a respecter of persons? Doesn't He feel the same way about your husband as He does about the whole world?

He loves your husband more than you do and wants Him to be obedient to the Word—for your husband's sake as well as yours. He sacrificed His only Son for truth to prevail in each of us. God cares! He really wants every good thing for us, having given everything that pertains to life and godliness through the knowledge of His Son, Jesus (see 2 Peter 1:3).

Peter also noted that our conversation was "coupled with fear." *Fear* means to be cautious, to beware, to act with the reverence produced by holy "fear" (*Vine's Expository Dictionary of Biblical Words*). God said the husband is the head of the marital relationship. When we reverence our husband as head, we show our love and respect both for God and our husband.

I've heard many women say, "You don't know my husband. These scriptures sound good, but they won't work for me."

First, we must have faith in God. "Now faith is the substance of things hoped for [*acting* like you have what you're hoping for], the evidence of things not seen [speaking as if you have what is not seen]" (Hebrews 11:1). It is the nature of faith to make its object real. Because we believe God and His Word, we act; that is, we do what God's Word says concerning our relationship with our husbands. Because we believe, we speak God's words to our husbands. We also pray God's Word back to God concerning our husbands, and we speak the Word of God about our husbands to them and to others. We speak God's Word concerning our husbands "coupled with fear." In an attitude of reverence, we respect who he is as a human being (God's creation) and as the head (God's assigned position for him in marriage). In reverence for God, we are obedient even when circumstances do not line up—a walk by faith not by sight. Faith sees the invisible, believes the incredible, receives the impossible.

When the famous missionary Hudson Taylor first went to China, he traveled in a sailing vessel. Close to the islands inhabited by cannibals, the ship was becalmed and slowly drifted toward the shore, unable to turn about. The savages were eagerly anticipating a feast.

The captain came to Taylor and besought him to pray for the help of God. "I will," said Taylor, "provided you set your sails to catch the breeze."

The captain declined to make himself a laughingstock by unfurling in a dead calm. Taylor said, "I will not undertake to pray for the vessel unless you will prepare the sails." And it was done.

While engaged in prayer, there was a knock at the door of Taylor's state room. "Who is there?" The captain's voice responded, "Are you still praying for wind?"

"Yes."

"Well," said the captain, "you'd better stop praying, for we have more wind than we can manage."

Faith without works is dead. We must pray to the Father and do what God's Word says. *Focus on obeying God by obeying your husband.* Trust God to make the change.

Works without faith are useless, and faith without works is dead. Faith and works (in that order) pulling together make for safety, progress and blessing.

The apostle also encouraged us to focus on incorruptible

things of the heart like the "ornament of a meek and quiet spirit" (1 Peter 3:4).

Meek means a "teachable" spirit—one that is approachable. A meek spirit is not an attitude of "I am more spiritual than you, and you can't tell me anything" but a humble one that reveals we are poor in spirit.

"Quiet" means a spirit without fear, full of faith, believing God in the face of adverse circumstances, continuing the work He has begun and finishing it. God is the author and finisher of our faith. "Quiet" doesn't mean we never say anything to our husbands; it's not a grin-and-bear-it attitude. It means passing on to your husband the same grace God has extended to you.

> As every man hath received the gift, even so minister the same one to another, as good stewards of the manifold grace of God. If any man speak, let him speak as the oracles of God; if any man minister, let him do it as of the ability which God giveth: that God in all things may be glorified through Jesus Christ, to whom be praise and dominion for ever and ever. Amen (1 Peter 4:10-11).

Here again we see stewardship in action: giving of that which God has given to us, laying down our lives for the man with whom we share great intimacy.

Can this be too much to ask of anyone? Jesus did it for us. God's Word says, "If we suffer, we shall also reign with him: if we deny him, he also will deny us" (2 Timothy 2:12).

"For if by one man's offence death reigned by one; much more they which receive abundance of grace and of the gift of righteousness shall reign in life by one, Jesus Christ" (Romans 5:17).

We must focus on lifting up the head (husband) and supporting him so he will not fall just as the Holy Spirit lifted up Jesus: "But when the Comforter is come, whom I will send unto you from the Father, even the Spirit of truth, which proceedeth from the Father, he shall testify of me" (John 15:26).

When the body of Christ lifts up Jesus, the Head, the body is lifted too. As wives lift up the marital head (our husbands), we are also lifted up.

We want to stay connected to the head, from which the whole body, supported and held together by its ligaments and sinews, grows as God causes it to grow.

Just as adverse life circumstances bring us to our knees and cause us to be keenly aware that our source for all things is God, so also adverse circumstances caused when our husbands make wrong decisions should bring us to our knees. Then we can find ourselves growing in faith, trust, patience and submission. Look how God uses our husbands to bless us!

Pleasing Your Husband

I wanted so much to be the perfect wife for Al that I wouldn't risk saying anything I thought might jeopardize our marriage. I feared he might leave me if I didn't say and do what he wanted me to. I feared what people would think of me, but more than that, I feared what my husband would think of me. I wanted to please Al more than I wanted to please God, although I didn't realize it much of my married life.

King Saul sinned in disobeying God. Samuel delivered a severe word from the Lord to him.

. . . Hath the Lord as great delight in burnt

offerings and sacrifices, as in obeying the voice of the Lord? Behold, to obey is better than sacrifice, and to hearken than the fat of rams. For rebellion is as the sin of witchcraft, and stubbornness is as iniquity and idolatry. Because thou hast rejected the word of the Lord, he hath also rejected thee from being king. And Saul said unto Samuel, I have sinned: for I have transgressed the commandment of the Lord, and thy words: *because I feared the people, and obeyed their voice* (1 Samuel 15:22-24, *italics added*).

When we go any way but God's way, our actions say we want to be in control. Like Adam and Eve, we are "trying to become as God." We imply we know better than God what is best for our lives. Scriptures say we thus enter into witchcraft (control), stubbornness that is as iniquity (to be strong in ourselves) and idolatry (allowing anyone or anything to come between us and God). This is a humanistic approach to life.

Instead of acting in fear that we will displease our husbands, let's be honest. When we don't feel good about certain things our husbands do that affect our lives, we should respectfully but honestly communicate it. We may be reluctant to express our concerns about spending, investing, disciplining the children or even how our husbands treat us. We may have real concerns over our husband's failure to consider the family's spiritual, health and emotional needs. Many marriages would even benefit from honest discussion about lovemaking. Communication is always vital for healthy relationships.

On the other hand, women who tend to talk too much and are not easily intimidated can be guilty of controlling their relationship. God advocates balance. In other words, we do not attempt to control our husbands nor do we suppress our need to communicate.

Can I love my husband enough to be his friend and tell him the truth, as God directs, with a meek and quiet spirit? Can I be patient while God does a work in his life to bring about change? Can I be a friend willing to lay down my life for my fellowman if my fellowman is my husband? Am I willing to be misunderstood to stand humbly for the truth?

We don't have to say everything that comes to mind. We don't have to release every emotion the moment we feel it. Our love is to be governed by truth, and our communication of truth is to be governed by love. We can be real and respond honestly with the right attitude of respect for our husbands.

If we fail to communicate and let negative feelings stew for a long time, we may suddenly find ourselves reacting emotionally. This should serve as a signal that we have an urgent need to communicate. Set aside a time to talk with your husband. Discover the source of the buildup of emotions. Forgive. Receive forgiveness. Be free again.

A wife's communication with her husband will actually serve to strengthen and bless him as long as she shares in a way he can receive. Sometimes when we have the best of intentions, the Holy Spirit will speak to us and reveal that our motivation is wrong. He shows us those places to which we are blind. Our reaction may be embarrassment, hurt, anger or defense. We may avoid listening to the voice of the Spirit. But He patiently waits for more opportunities to show us until we receive His message.

You can expect your husband to react with some of these same feelings and responses to you, especially when you are dealing with negatives that require change. You will be tempted to protect his feelings, to take back what was said, to apologize. Instead, wait on the Lord. Trust God to work in your husband the way He chooses. In the meantime, intercede for him. Be willing to ask your husband to forgive you for anything God shows you about yourself. Give your husband the opportunity to become responsible in the areas you were led to communicate to him. He will feel much better about himself, and he will experience more fulfillment as a man. You will experience more of what it means to be his helpmeet through these areas of difficulty and times of change.

Broken Commitment

God the Father responded to the prayer of Jesus and sent the Holy Spirit to abide with us forever (see John 14:16). He will not leave us unless we consistently make Him unwelcome. David realized the sensitivity of the Holy Spirit. Because of his sins, David pleaded with God not to take the Holy Spirit from him (see Psalm 51).

Similarly, when we joined our husbands in matrimony, we made the commitment "till death do us part." Our intentions were to dwell with him forever. God's desire for us to remain together is clearly stated in the Word, but He does make room for another way if there is absolutely no way two people can live together. He urges us to try to reconcile although He allows divorce in circumstances of infidelity and certain kinds of abuse.

Some wives have suffered such abuse that leaving is the only way they can survive. When these victims and God have reached such a decision, we must not add insult to injury. Our place as fellow believers is to minister love and encouragement to all victims of broken marriages. The body of Christ owes them not rejection but compassion and intercession.

God never gives up on anyone. Our ministry to victims of separation or divorce can help restore them to strength and wholeness in Christ. Then they can spend time interceding for their husbands to experience a supernatural change. Otherwise, they may lose not only their families but also their souls.

Intercession is perhaps the greatest way any woman can bless and help her husband. God has given us the opportunity to communicate constantly with Him. This gives us hope for our marriage, hope that our husbands will change and hope that we too will be changed.

> For we are saved by hope: but hope that is seen is not hope: for what a man seeth, why doth he yet hope for? But if we hope for that we see not, then do we with patience wait for it. Likewise the Spirit also helpeth our infirmities: for we know not what we should pray for as we ought: but the Spirit itself maketh intercession for us with groanings which cannot be uttered. And he that searcheth the hearts knoweth what is the mind of the Spirit, because he maketh intercession for the saints according to the will of God (Romans 8:24-27).

Called to Intercede

Years ago Al and I had some very deep needs I had prayed about for a long time, with no indication my prayers were getting anywhere. I had come to know the importance of praying in the Spirit when needs couldn't be put into words but had not reached the place I could easily and comfortably pray in tongues, or allow the "Spirit to make intercession." The only time I could pray in tongues was when I was, as Pentecostals refer to it, "receiving a blessing." Yet I was developing a greater hunger for God and a compelling desire to intercede in the Spirit.

I accompanied Al on a trip to Alabama where he was to speak at a church pastored by Sister Mary Graves. Sunday morning Sister Graves received a phone call from a lady seeking directions to the church. She also wanted to confirm that this was where the Al Taylor advertised in the newspaper would be speaking.

After the morning service, I overheard the lady say she had been called to be an intercessor. God gave her names of people she didn't know, and she interceded for them in the Spirit. Sometimes God also gave her the face with the name. She had been interceding for an Al Taylor. She had come to see if this was the man whose name and face God had shown her; he was. She also felt God released her that day from the call to intercede for him.

I cannot tell you how grieved I was in my spirit when I realized God had raised up someone my husband didn't even know to intercede in the Spirit for him. When I returned home, I sought the Lord diligently. Not many days passed before I was able to pray in the Spirit not only for Al but for others too. I felt led of God to spend at least an hour each day interceding for my husband both in the understanding (in English) and in the Spirit. By the end of two years, we could see the hand of God moving in a major way to break enemy strongholds in our lives.

Many times I was tempted to stop my intercession. I found getting up each morning harder and harder. But as I renewed my mind according to Romans 8:24-27, God gave me strength. My hope gradually became more centered on God than on my prayers. Realizing the Holy Spirit knew what to pray increased my hope, and I didn't give up. Although I spent most of my prayer time interceding for my husband, I began to see God making significant changes in me.

Through prayer I began to experience greater love for my husband. I began more often to see beyond his faults to his needs. Rather than be discouraged by his needs, I took them to the Father. The Holy Spirit gave me a greater understanding of my husband as He gave me discernment. During those two years, the time between the coming forth of the blade until the corn was in the ear seemed long (see Mark 4:28). But God was patiently at work in both Al and me to produce change. Although God's deliverance came to us years ago, we struggled from time to time to live and walk in that deliverance.

Hope keeps us through every situation. The Holy Spirit prays the will of God for our lives. The Word of God is true. Women can be ever so thankful to God for the powerful opportunities to be helpmeets for our husbands. While we intercede for them, we are both being changed.

> And this is the confidence that we have in him, that, if we ask any thing according to his will, he heareth us; and if we know that he hears us, whatsoever we ask, we know that we have the petitions that we desired of him (1 John 5:14, 15).

What better way to deal with our problems than to give them to the One who made us!

What comfort to know we don't have to change our husbands or try to make them do the changing! What a comfort to know there is hope for our marriages through Jesus Christ our Lord! What better way to help our husbands!

What a tremendous hope for our husbands to be free to be what God has called them to be! When they are free from the weights that beset them, they will be more confident in their roles as head of the marriage. As they begin opening up to receive God's grace, they will have more grace to extend to us. We cannot lose. As we show our husbands acceptance by taking their needs to God, we are no longer compelled to condemn, judge and accuse them. That leaves our husbands free to accept us in spite of our peculiarities. We cannot give ourselves in prayer and love without eventually receiving the investment multiplied and returned to us. That return blesses us and our children.

Standing Invitation

We are invited to come to the table of Jesus Christ and partake freely of the Bread of Life. This standing invitation for every believer is represented by the table of shewbread. Accepting this invitation allows us the privilege to fill our minds with the Word of God and daily increase our knowledge of the Father through fellowship with Christ. The mind is the gateway to the heart (or spirit of man). Therefore, partaking of the Lord's table by feeding on His Word is the only means whereby we can change and strengthen our hearts.

Developing a strong appetite for the Word of God and delighting in fellowship with the Lord produces changes in us that qualify us for the next step of intimacy. Similarly, as we receive with delight all that our husbands have to give as head of our marriage, we will experience healthy growth as the body. Walking in an attitude of obedience, giving respect and honor to our husbands, makes us ready for greater intimacy in our marriage relationship too.

Love: God's Gift

Love doesn't remove the burden,
    It just helps one carry the load!
Love doesn't narrow life's path . . .
    It makes an even broader road.
Love doesn't make one blind,
    It lets one see more to do.
Love is not black and white,
    It's shades of pink and blue!

Love is a gift of God
    Quite rare . . . its true.
And, unworthy though we are,
    It's given to me and you!

—Cheryl Justice

Chapter Six

Cooperation—Holy Spirit

FOURTH STEP TO INTIMACY—CANDLESTICK

Full Acceptance of Our Roles

The golden candlestick, or lampstand, symbolizes the work of the Holy Spirit to enlighten and empower the Church. The corresponding Feast of Pentecost dramatized the time when the Holy Spirit would come to baptize believers and indwell the Church by His power and fullness.

In Matthew 3:11 John the Baptist said, "I indeed baptize you with water unto repentance: but he that cometh after me is mightier than I, whose shoes I am not worthy to bear: he shall baptize you with the Holy Ghost, and with fire." Luke noted in Acts that "we are his witnesses of these things; and so is also the Holy Ghost, whom God hath given to them that obey him" (Acts 5:32).

God gives the Holy Spirit to those who obey Him and immerses our lives *in* the Holy Spirit. This is the key to the Spirit-led life. We can live and walk in the Spirit. We are energized by Him to do all that Christ commands.

This is a vital step of victory. The "Word" presented on

the table of shewbread and the "Holy Spirit" symbolized by the oil and fire of the candlestick are a powerful pair. The "Word" and "Spirit" each fully accept their own role and the role of the other. They act as one in total, perfect agreement. The "Word," who is Jesus Christ the Head, accepts that the "Holy Spirit" is necessary to help Him carry out His work.

This is an example to us of the power of agreement in the union of husband and wife. As the husband and wife each fully accept their own role and that of the other, they begin to act as one in agreement. The husband as head accepts that the wife, who is his body, is necessary to help him to carry out the desires and goals for their lives together.

The husband is fulfilled, living in the pattern of Jesus Christ. The wife delights in living in the pattern of the Holy Spirit. The biblical balance of their union is a revelation to the world of Christ and the Church.

From Christ the preeminent One comes direction and sustenance to the Church. This enables the church to grow, reproduce and be a blessing. Just as the main shaft of the candlestick is the source of oil for all the branches, the husband stands tall with the branches of his family beside him. He has a substantial responsibility to supply his family with direction and sustenance.

Holy Spirit

The candlestick is the most ornate of all the tabernacle furniture and provides several symbols of the Holy Spirit. The oil, the flame and the illumination represent vital elements of the Holy Spirit in the ministry of Christ.

The Feast of Pentecost was a type of the Holy Spirit in the Old Testament. This feast anticipated the coming of the Holy Spirit in fullness on the Day of Pentecost. The Holy Spirit's outpouring followed Christ's sacrifice on Calvary during

Passover, fifty days after the Feast of Firstfruits.

The Bible offers us much understanding regarding the Holy Spirit. This understanding will help us in our quest for spiritual intimacy with God. The Holy Spirit *is* God. He is equal with the Father and the Son. He is one with the Father and the Son. He is neither more important nor less important than the other members of the Godhead.

The Holy Spirit came to dwell in our bodies: "What? know ye not that your body is the temple of the Holy Ghost which is in you, which ye have of God, and ye are not your own?" (1 Corinthians 6:19). The Church is the body of Christ, and when the Holy Spirit dwells in us individually, He dwells in the Church. He came to indwell us when the Father sent Him. This was after Jesus prayed to the Father to send the Comforter and paid the purchase price for His bride, the Church.

The body of believers constitutes the physical dwelling place of the Holy Spirit. Likewise, the wife is the body of her husband in marriage.

> So ought men to love their wives as their own bodies. He that loveth his wife loveth himself. For no man every yet hated his own flesh; but nourisheth and cherisheth it, even as the Lord the church. For we are members of his body, of his flesh, and of his bones. For this cause shall a man leave his father and mother and shall be joined unto his wife, and they two shall be one flesh (Ephesians 5:28-31).

The physical body and its functions give us a clear picture of our roles as the body of Christ and as the body of our husbands. The body takes food received through the head, then breaks it down through digestion to give life and energy to both the head *and* the body. The Holy Spirit is responsible for taking the Word given by Christ and breaking it down for the body (both the Church and the individual believer).

Respecting Our Husbands

As the candlestick consumes the olive oil, it produces light for the sanctuary (the Holy Place). It illuminates the table of shewbread, the golden altar (altar of incense) and itself. Similarly, we are to be witnesses of Jesus through the energizing oil of the Spirit. The Holy Spirit always illuminates Jesus and His Word in all He does in us and in the Church. "But when the Comforter is come, whom I will send unto you from the Father, even the Spirit of truth, which proceedeth from the Father, he shall testify of me" (John 15:26).

Wives are commanded to support our husbands similarly: ". . . And the wife see that she reverence her husband" (Ephesians 5:33). For us, this is like supplying fuel to the fire in our husbands' lives—they are truly energized.

Reverence (*phobeo*) means "to fear." This is not simple fear but reverence whereby an individual recognizes the power and position of the individual revered and renders him proper respect. Our husbands, of course, are not gods, nor are we to treat them as such. We are to show honor and respect to them as the head of our relationship. A head needs the support of a body. It cannot fulfill its responsibility without it. Neither can the body without the head.

Husbands need all the encouragement, inspiration and appreciation we can give them. Our communication to them and about them should always reveal our respect for them, even when we must confront negative aspects of our relationship.

Communicating Respectfully

As individuals we might ask ourselves:

•What do I communicate? Do I communicate sincere interest in my husband's welfare?
•Do I show interest in his pursuits?
•Do I talk about his day and what is important to him?
•Do I listen to him without interrupting? Do I show respect by the way I act and the things I say?
•Do I reflect an attitude that says, "I truly want to know you, and I want you to know me the same way"?
•Do I confirm that I understand clearly what he is saying, or do I argue without knowing for sure what he was saying?
•Do I listen with my heart?
•Do I display an attitude of judgment, accusation or condemnation?
•Do I sometimes belittle him when he is gentle, tender or emotional?
•Do I dwell on his negatives more than his positives?
•Do I try to share encouraging words every day?
•Do my mannerisms reveal ugly attitudes like impatience?
•Do I believe my husband can do all things through Christ?
•Do I manipulate him through words, emotions or attitudes?

If we have trouble supporting our husband as our head, we must go to the Father in prayer and ask Him to show us our problem and deliver us from it.

Remember, when we lift up our husbands, we are also lifted up. We become blessed because we are a blessing. We may not see fruit immediately, but it will come if we are persistent. God will take care of us and fulfill His promises to us.

What I have just described fits under the woman's role as "supporter" to her husband. These are some ways through which we can lift up the head. To our husbands, it is a part of the blessing of comfort and nurture received through our being loving wives.

Respect Through Patience

One characteristic of the Holy Spirit is that He respects us individually. He never forces Himself on us. He doesn't force us to listen or do any of the things He would like us to do. All the fruit of the Spirit are clearly manifested by the Holy Spirit, and that fruit is evident in every relationship with Him. He is gentle, loving, compassionate and longsuffering toward us. He always brings to us goodness, and the goodness of the Lord leads men to repentance (see Romans 2:4).

Wives can emulate this beautiful characteristic of the Holy Spirit. We can show respect for our husbands by not attempting to force or manipulate them to do what we want. We can communicate our needs to them with love and then trust God to work in them to bring forth that which agrees with His Word. We can bless our husbands and have "good days" because we obey the instruction in 1 Peter 3:10: "For he that will love life, and see *good days*, let him refrain his tongue from evil, and his lips that they speak no guile" (*italics added*).

The following scriptures open our understanding to proper conduct and conversation in the Spirit-led life:

Death and life are in the power of the tongue: and they that love it shall eat the fruit thereof (Proverbs 18:21).

Whoso keepeth his mouth and his tongue keepeth his soul from troubles (Proverbs 21:23).

A word fitly spoken is like apples of gold in pictures of silver (Proverbs 25:11).

Every word of God is pure: he is a shield unto them that put their trust in him. Add thou not unto his words, lest he reprove thee, and thou be found a liar (Proverbs 30:5-6).

Hear counsel, and receive instruction, that thou mayest be wise in thy latter end (Proverbs 19:20).

If we pattern our lives after the Holy Spirit, we will speak things that edify:

Let no corrupt communication proceed out of your mouth, but that which is good to the use of edifying, that it may minister grace to the hearers. And grieve not the holy Spirit of God, whereby ye are sealed unto the day of redemption. Let all bitterness, and wrath, and anger, and clamour, and evil speaking, be put away from you, with all malice (Ephesians 4:29-31).

We need to watch for anything that might compete with our loyalty to Jesus. Likewise, we must watch for anything that would compete with our loyalty to our husbands. The greatest competitor of devotion to Jesus is often our service to Him; the same can happen in the marriage relationship.

We can be aware of all the things we do for our husbands: cooking his meals, cleaning, washing and ironing his clothes, putting up things he leaves out, making calls for him, perhaps cutting his hair, doing special favors and meaningful gestures. But are we aware of what our words and attitudes do to him?

We cannot substitute activities for personal, intimate relationship. Our goal is intimacy . . . a fundamental need for both of us. Intimacy can be achieved as we more fully accept and relate to each other by patterning after the way Jesus and the Holy Spirit accept and relate to each other without competition. The marriage relationship provides opportunity to improve our attitudes, understanding and communication. This helps prepare us for better, more effective communication with our Father in heaven.

The union of Word and Spirit brings forth new life. The joining of the Holy Spirit with Christ enabled Him to purchase the Church. He was beaten for her. That is why God required the golden candlestick to be constructed of pure, beaten gold— it typified the ordeal of Christ during His time of sacrifice.

The oil of the candlestick was made from olives. Olives were continually crushed to provide oil so the candlestick could burn perpetually. Only after Jesus was crushed was the Holy Spirit released to abide with us forever. This olive oil symbolizes the Holy Spirit in the Church, flowing from Christ to us to burn out impurities, to produce the fruit of righteousness and to illuminate truth.

Responder

A significant part of the woman's role in marriage is to respond to the initiatives of the husband. This pattern is established during courtship in most marriages. The roles originated with the Creator consistent with His plan for our lives. When we do not follow the roles set forth in God's Word, confusion and division are produced in our relationships. This kind of rebellion to the commands of God results in pain, frustration and chaos and presents to our children an image contrary to God's plan.

The Holy Spirit is a responder. In creation the Holy Spirit awaits the Word and then acts upon it and in full accordance with it. He acts upon the truths Jesus taught. He is here to work with us in response to the Father's command. He is a brilliant and patient teacher. He overshadows the Word we receive to bring it to fruition in our lives. He gently nudges us to accept His guidance.

For example, if I am determined to watch a particular television program but don't really feel comfortable with what I see, I tell myself, "There's nothing wrong with this. Many of my Christian friends watch this program." I tune out the uncomfortable feeling and in reality tune out the Holy Spirit so I can fulfill the lusts of my flesh. I rationalize by telling myself the Holy Spirit came to comfort me, not make me uncomfortable. True comfort, however, only comes from the Holy Spirit as I cooperate by not allowing those things into my life that grieve Him. He resists those things that bring death in my spirit. The Holy Spirit is pro-life in the full sense of the term. He loves us enough to respond honestly to everything in our lives.

Like the Holy Spirit, many times we don't feel good about some things our husbands do or some things to which they expose themselves. We can't always explain it, but we know in our spirit something is wrong. We must love our husbands enough to share our responses and leave them to determine if they should change their actions. If they do not take heed immediately, we have, as we discussed earlier, the opportunity to intercede to the Father until changes are made in their hearts. A change in their hearts will bring change in their actions.

Respecting by Responding in Love

Only one time does the New Testament command wives to love their husbands, and even then the command is indirect and not the same word God uses in commanding husbands to love their wives. Women are responders and will usually respond to *agape* love from their husbands by giving *agape* love; that is, the God kind of love in return.

> The aged women likewise, that they be in behaviour as becometh holiness, not false accusers, not given to much wine, teachers of good things; that they may teach the young women to be sober, to *love their husbands*, to love their children, to be discreet, chaste, keepers at home, good, obedient to their own husbands, that the word of God be not blasphemed (Titus 2:3-5, *italics added*).

The word *love* in this text is *phileo*. It is used toward man, never toward God. It indicates friendship love and requires honest communication. Such a requirement can be challenging to women who are easily intimidated. Some husbands feel threatened by honest communication, especially if it contains any negatives about them.

A woman is tempted to not express her feelings if her husband is likely to misunderstand. Thus, deception begins to work in the marriage. To prevent his becoming upset, she may say she is happy when she is sad, that she feels good when she feels bad, even that she likes his bad habits just to please him.

The enemy will tell her this is the way to keep peace.

Such surface "peace" isn't real, nor can it last. Problems don't get solved with this deceptive approach. The opportunity for change gets buried under pretense. The marriage becomes a miserable rut. Problems pile up until the husband and wife often become alienated. As tension mounts, they eventually find themselves exploding over silly things that don't even relate to the real problem. Communication becomes lost because real communication must be based on truth.

For many years my communication was suppressed because I hadn't learned to open up. I never felt free to offer my opinion nor confident enough to take responsibility for it. I carried much hurt, fear, anger and unforgiveness for what was happening in my life.

After Al and I were married, I continued to suppress my feelings. When after many years I finally began to open up, he had a difficult time believing the things I shared from my heart. Because so much time had elapsed, he didn't remember some incidents to which I referred. He had trouble determining whether I was being honest. *Had I been honest when he didn't know I was suppressing my feelings? Was I being honest now? Or was I simply imagining all of this?* He wanted to believe the early years of our marriage represented the truth because our relationship *seemed* much smoother then. Of course, it wasn't; it only appeared that way because I rarely said anything contrary to what he was saying or questioned anything he did. I thought if I were truly submissive, I would never disagree with him. The few times I voiced my opinion, I felt so guilty I soon asked him to forgive me. Such incidents reinforced his control over me and encouraged him to continue.

My response to Al essentially said, "Forgive me for not having the same opinion as you." In reality, I idolized him, acting as if he could never be wrong and I could never be right. Yet down deep inside I felt I was not always wrong.

Consequently, I began to resent the control I allowed him to have over me.

Al and I never considered divorce. Our commitment to each other was strong. That, coupled with our desire to obey the Lord, held us together. In extreme cases some couples need to go their separate ways, but God's ideal for us was in our vows: "What God has joined together, let no man put asunder." Even in extremely difficult cases, I believe God wants couples to make *every possible effort* to rebuild and come together again after restoration.

Humbling myself to respond honestly to my husband was difficult, even after I learned about it from the Bible. Dealing with the pride in my life has taken time, and that pride would not allow me to be real like the butterfly. Being *real* meant revealing myself, and verbal communication has always been a weak area of my life. I felt I never knew how to "properly" ask questions or even how to formulate them. God has given my husband a great deal of patience in this area, and I am thankful. His patience is giving me time to learn, change and grow.

I have not always understood how to speak the truth in love. For a long time I thought that because I loved my husband, the *way* I communicated with him should never be a barrier to his receiving my words. However, this did not alter the fact that communicating the wrong way was indeed a barrier.

That we henceforth be no more children, tossed to and fro, and carried about with every wind of doctrine, by the sleight of men, and cunning craftiness, whereby they lie in wait to deceive; but *speaking the truth in love*, may grow up into him in all things, which is the head, even Christ. From whom the whole body fitly joined together and compacted by that which every joint supplieth, according to the effectual working in the measure of every part, maketh increase of the body into the edifying of itself in love (Ephesians 4:14-16, *italics added*).

"Open rebuke is better than secret love. Faithful are the wounds of a friend; but the kisses of an enemy are deceitful" (Proverbs 27:5-6).

God is taking away the fear I have had of communicating with Al and is giving me *more* strength to speak the truth in love. He is helping me to more boldly share my heart with Al, for I fear God more than man.

When we willingly receive the illuminating ministry of the Holy Spirit, we see clearly the table of shewbread, the golden candlestick and the golden altar. The Holy Spirit illumines through the burning of the olive oil in the Golden Candlestick. Women literally illumine these same spiritual truths to our husbands and children as the Holy Spirit shines through us. All we do should be as unto the Lord. Fulfilling our God-given roles provides opportunity for us to share the spiritual parallel with our families. Our daily preparation of bread and nourishment hearkens back to the Holy Spirit's role to "give us this day our daily bread." Just as Christ is our spiritual bread and nourishment served to us by the Holy Spirit, so we prepare nourishment to serve our families.

John Sims says in *Power With Purpose* that "the doctrine of the Holy Spirit is one of Christianity's most abused doctrines." On the day the Holy Spirit arrived at the first Pentecost after Jesus' resurrection, those who had received the Holy Spirit baptism were accused of being drunk. Today many say the speaking-in-tongues manifestation is of the devil. Other gifts of the Spirit are attributed to emotionalism. Many churches quench the Spirit by suppressing any manifestation of the Spirit. Some believers have been taught not to receive Him in His fullness. Others want the gifts of the Spirit but are unwilling to bear the fruit of the Spirit. Still others covet the gifts and manifestations of the Spirit but ignore or resist the Holy Spirit's work of conviction and cleansing.

I believe God wants us to accept fully the Holy Spirit in all His manifestations. Whether they are gifts, fruit, tongues, guidance, teaching, drawing, convicting or cleansing, all should be accepted by us. We are not to pick and choose what we will or won't accept. The choice is not ours. All are part of the Holy Spirit. If we reject His manifestations, we reject the Holy Spirit.

Many women cry out to their husbands for understanding. They want their husbands to take time to know how they were created by God to function as a female. They know then that their husbands can more easily honor, respect and understand them.

> Likewise, ye husbands, dwell with them according to knowledge, giving honour unto the wife, as unto the weaker [more sensitive, easily broken] vessel, and as being heirs together of the grace of life; that your prayers be not hindered (1 Peter 3:7).

Some women are aware that their femininity is not fully accepted by their husbands. Others only know they are frustrated. Some reach out to other men for acceptance. Vulnerable to almost any man who shows understanding for their emotional needs, they often give themselves in physical intimacy to the person who offered emotional intimacy.

Husbands frequently emphasize sexual intimacy more

than relational intimacy. For sex, some will change schedules, miss appointments, take the phone off the hook; but for communication—that is, baring his heart to his wife or allowing his wife to bare her heart to him—he has no time. Because he works hard to provide for her physical needs, husbands commonly express the attitude, "What more do you want from me?" Of course, such a husband displays great shock when discovering his ungrateful wife has had an affair.

Women usually relate to the tendency of men to pursue them for what they want physically while rejecting them for who they really are. This has produced dislocation and dysfunction in marriage and family. However, as women we have the opportunity to counter this abuse by focusing on Jesus while lifting up our husbands. We will be quickened and made more alive than we can possibly imagine.

Discern the Body's Sensitivities

The apostle Paul charged the church at Corinth with failure to "discern the body." That same failure creates crisis in the Church and calamity in marriages.

> For he that eateth and drinketh unworthily, eateth and drinketh damnation to himself, not discerning the Lord's body. For this cause many are weak and sickly among you, and many sleep [have died] (1 Corinthians 11:29).

If husbands do not take the time to honor wives in our weakness (the tender, sensitive areas of our emotions that are easily broken), they will become weak themselves (accepting the world's false definitions of manhood). They will suffer the infirmity of being unable to read their own feelings. They will be unable to deal with their family and meet their emotional needs. Thus, their own emotional needs cannot be met. They will be much more likely to die prematurely because of failure to discern the body (the wife God provided for them).

The Church illustrates many truths about marriage and family. Conversely, marriage and family illustrate many truths essential to the Church. Each man who discerns the Church as the body of Christ and discerns our Lord's great gift of His own human body for the Church is ready to understand his own relationship to his wife. When men see God's provision for their own spiritual, emotional, physical and intellectual needs, they can better hear God's call for them to lay down their lives for their wives as Christ did. They can grasp a woman's need for relationship, including continual heart-to-heart communication.

This essential step of marital intimacy constitutes moving from head knowledge to heart knowledge. Before men can deal with what is hidden in their hearts, they must first get in touch with their own feelings.

Until a man receives the provisions Christ has made to meet his own emotional needs, he is unable to understand his wife and her needs. Just as church leaders must judge themselves so they do not have to be judged by their followers, similarly the husband must judge himself so his wife and family will not need to judge him.

Providing all the outward comforts for the body (that which feels good, tastes good, looks good, smells good and sounds good) without providing for the body's emotional, spiritual and true physical needs is another failure to discern the body. A body can exist in such a condition, but it is deprived of the joy that comes with inner strength and beauty. An excess of creature comforts may actually serve to obstruct a person's realization of how empty and wretched he or she is inside. The church at Laodicea demonstrated this malady (see Colossians

2:1, 10, 17; Revelation 3:17).

As we become aware of our husbands' needs in any of these areas, we are called by God to intercede to the Father until those needs are met. While we are in prayer, we can be open to whatever God may show us about ourselves as we keep in mind that God is not finished with us either.

Some women have not yet recognized that an unhealthy focus on the external (the body more than the spirit) produces frustration and a lack of self-worth in the marriage. Both partners are likely to bring this confusion into the marriage. When they do, problems will compound rapidly.

> For if we would judge ourselves, we should not
> be judged. But when we are judged, we are chastened
> of the Lord, that we should not be condemned with
> the world (1 Corinthians 11:31-32).

God has provided everything we need in our inner person to make the outer person strong, blessed and healthy (see 3 John 2). If we judge ourselves and repent, God will forgive us and not have to chasten us. If we do not judge ourselves, our bodies—through mental or physical problems—will eventually reveal to us that something is awry. Yet we will not be condemned with the world when we repent, reform and receive God's forgiveness. The world may do the same things, but they lack relationship with God. They neither are chastened nor do they repent. They continue on the same path until they are destroyed.

Like us, our husbands are imperfect people with human needs that can only be met as we are obedient to Christ's instructions. We are the channels God has chosen to meet certain needs no other person can legitimately meet. We can more easily follow the pattern of the Holy Spirit when we accept the call to be God's chosen channel of blessing. Then we can focus more attention on loving and caring for the head. He will then become strong enough to love and care for us in our uniquely feminine ways.

Our husbands must become ever mindful of the sowing and reaping principle in our marriages. Wives multiply everything sown into their lives—good or bad. Husbands who initiate good things reap a harvest of blessing. Husbands who sow works of the flesh reap a harvest of misery.

Notice God commands the woman before the man, children before the parents, slaves before the masters and citizens before government (see Ephesians 5:22-33, 6:1-9; Colossians 3:18-25; 1 Peter 2:13-3:1). Unless we submit, the head cannot govern. It is good to be the body. It is all right to give, to suffer, to receive direction, even to go with the head in the wrong direction for a while as you trust God to change him. A woman can be submissive to the head and still communicate honestly with him. She can be sensitive and emotional. The body can even enjoy the provisions and blessings the head gives. She can also enjoy being different from her husband. God created us and established the order of this relationship.

God understands that women's needs and desires are unique to us as the bodies of our husbands. He made us this way. We do not dishonor Him by becoming aware of our needs and desires.

But as the bodies of our husbands, we seek acceptance just as the Holy Spirit seeks acceptance. As the Holy Spirit wants to be embraced and reassured of our love, so wives want to be embraced and reassured of their husband's love. The Holy Spirit desires that we show Him respect by appreciating His sensitivities, which provide guidance for our lives. We also desire that our husbands show respect for us by appreciating our sensitivities, which help to provide guidance for our marriage.

The Holy Spirit wants us to be mindful of His work in our lives that brings forth fruit. We too want our husbands to be mindful of our work that helps bring forth fruit in their lives.

The Holy Spirit desires that we give careful attention to and consider valuable His communication or responses to us, even if we don't agree with them. Likewise, we want our husbands to give careful attention to and consider valuable our communication or responses to them, whether or not we agree.

The Holy Spirit desires that we not make decisions without first hearing from Him. We want our husbands to include us in the decision-making process by hearing what we have to offer concerning any decisions that need to be made.

The Holy Spirit wants us to acknowledge His ability to comfort, intercede, teach and guide our lives. We want our husbands to acknowledge our ability to comfort them, intercede for them, teach our children, guide the home *and* live a godly life.

The Holy Spirit would like us to reveal by our actions *and* words that we need Him; therefore, we are not better off without Him. We want our husbands to reveal in their actions and words that they need us and are better off with us.

The Holy Spirit can be provoked (Psalm 106:33), vexed (Isaiah 63:10), grieved (Ephesians 4:30), quenched (1 Thessalonians 5:19) and blasphemed (Matthew 12:31-33). So too our husbands can provoke, vex, grieve, quench and blaspheme us.

But God understands our needs and has a plan.

When we do not experience full acceptance by our husbands, we have a way of escape through intercession and living the Word. Communication of the body to the head is necessary, but communication to the Father in the Spirit is vital for life. Both are necessary to be complete.

Intercession takes place at the golden altar, which we will discuss in the next chapter, where we come to also hear from the Almighty who knows all things and takes our situations seriously. Intercession secures the help of God in opening the channels of communication with our husbands. One way to open these channels is through giving our needs to Him. We then receive grace to give to our husbands the very things we need from them. The Golden Rule always applies: "And as ye would that men should do to you, do ye also to them likewise" (Luke 6:31).

According to Zechariah 12:10 and Hebrews 10:29, grace comes through the Holy Spirit. Let us be channels, like the Spirit, through which grace flows to our husbands. When we want to follow the scriptural pattern for wives, we can be filled with the oil and fire of the Spirit. We can make our husbands glad as in the Song of Solomon: "How fair is thy love, my sister, my spouse! how much better is thy love than wine!" (Song of Solomon 4:10) As we cooperate with God's plan for unity with our husbands, our hearts are prepared for intercession.

Love

It's true . . . I love you . . .
Not for a moment, but forever.
Feelings are fickle . . . love is constant.
Constantly count on my love.

—*Cheryl Justice*

Chapter Seven

Cooperation—Prayers

FIFTH STEP TO INTIMACY—GOLDEN ALTAR

Communication

In the Holy Place is the golden altar, the place we express to God our love and devotion in the name of Jesus by the power of the Spirit. This step gets us in position to hear *from* God.

Only when the body of Christ fully accepts Jesus and the Holy Spirit are they ready to come to the golden altar. The fire on the golden altar always came from the brazen altar, and the blood the priest sprinkled on the altar came from the sacrifice made on the brazen altar. The priest was instructed to burn only incense designated by God on this altar. No undesignated incense, no sacrifice, neither meat offering nor drink offerings could be offered here. The burning incense symbolized prayer rising up to God. Psalm 141:2 says, "Let my prayer be set forth before thee as incense. . . ."

The Feast of Trumpets corresponds with the golden altar. This feast was a memorial of blowing trumpets to call the children of Israel to assemble at the door of the tabernacle of the congregation (see Numbers 10:3). The purpose of the feast was for the people to prepare to hear from God by physically coming to a specific place where they could hear God's message through His servant.

The golden altar was centered immediately before the veil to the Most Holy Place. This means it was in front of the mercy seat and the ark of the covenant located just beyond the veil.

"And thou shalt make an altar to burn incense upon. . . . And thou shalt put it before the veil that is by the ark of the testimony, before the mercy seat that is over the testimony, where I will meet with thee" (Exodus 30:1, 6).

Leviticus 4:7 and 18 refer to the golden altar as "the altar which is before the Lord."

The golden altar and the Feast of Trumpets were symbolic of worship. This worship was *true* worship that would usher the worshiper into the very presence of God behind the veil in the Most Holy Place.

We can come to the golden altar because of the blood of Jesus (symbolized by the blood from the sacrifice sprinkled on the golden altar) that has been applied to our lives. Because we have received Christ's provision—the sacrifice at the brazen altar, the perpetual cleansing of the laver, the nourishment of the table of shewbread, and the light and energy of the golden candlestick—we are prepared to come to the golden altar in true worship.

> But the hour cometh, and now is, when the true worshippers shall worship the Father in spirit and in truth: for the Father seeketh such to worship Him. God is a Spirit: and they that worship him must worship him in Spirit and in truth (John 4:23-24).

The light of the Holy Spirit shows us the truth of God's Word (Jesus) enabling and empowering us to apply it to our life situations daily.

True worshipers will not come to give mere lip service. We will have the Word written on the table of our hearts and will live it out in our daily walk.

True worshipers are symbolized by specific incense and its burning. The incense represented truth being spoken to God by the worshiper. Its burning represented the energizing of that truth in the heart and life of the worshiper. The smoke that rose up to God was truth spoken out of the heart of the worshiper to God. The Holy Spirit moved on the Word (Jesus) to create this sweet fragrance.

By the power of the Spirit we come in Jesus' name. This is a step of humility, recognizing that only because we are in covenant with Jesus (symbolized by the blood on the altar) can we take this step of intimacy with God.

We do not come to God because of our good works— "God, You know I've been a good neighbor. I've visited people in the hospital. I've been a faithful wife and a loving mother. I've taught Sunday school and led people to worship you." Good works do not give us access to the throne of God.

Our *performance* or self-righteousness will not give us access to God's presence. Nor can we enter His presence with an attitude that says "I sacrificed time with my family to give godly counsel to a friend for You, God" or "I sacrificed the new home I wanted so badly to give that money to missions." Our *sacrifices* are not sufficient to bring us to the throne room.

We cannot come into His presence based on our spiritual *experiences*. Visions, dreams, casting out demons or believing for another's healing will not give us access to the throne room.

Only the work of Jesus and *His performance* of giving

His best, His all, His life, is sufficient! Only *His blood sacrifice* through dying, which was *His experience* at the Cross, is adequate! Because we receive Jesus as Lord of our lives, we receive His cleansing blood. This gives us access to the throne room of Father God. In the name of our precious Lord and Savior, we can come boldly to our Father. Because Jesus paid a ransom for us, we have this blessed privilege of union in fellowship with the Father!

Only to the extent we have received the knowledge of the truth (Jesus) can we surrender to the Holy Spirit to make that truth come alive in us. When our attitude is one of coming to God in Jesus' name by the power of the Spirit, we are ushered into God's presence. This daily process will draw us ever closer to God to abide forever in His presence.

With a heart of thanksgiving we take our step of intimacy to bless the Lord of glory. We praise Him for His mighty acts because He has blessed His creation mightily. We praise Him for His excellent greatness because of who He is! We extol His magnificent majesty spontaneously! We express our love and admiration to Abba Father! Our focus is not on what He can do for us but on who He is—our Creator, our source of life!

We give out of our hearts all He has made possible in us. We give Him glory and strength. We praise and honor Him, the Almighty Holy Father. We extol this the only true God, the perfect, gracious, loving Father, for who He is. We acknowledge His awesome majesty. We bless Him with all that is within us. We praise him in the song and dance (see Psalm 150:4). We praise him with musical instruments (see Psalm 150). We praise Him with uplifted hands symbolizing complete surrender (Psalm 141:2).

"I will therefore that men pray every where, lifting up holy hands, without wrath and doubting" (1 Timothy 2:8). Trouble raising our hands in this manner may indicate that something hinders our full surrender. If so, we can allow God to search our hearts and show us the barrier. Once we have given it to Him, we can worship Him freely.

Any praise that's been given to us, we give to the Father. Any compliments, appreciation, love or friendship, we give to the Father. We give them so they won't stay in our lives to bring satisfaction to our flesh. If we don't pour them out to God, they will become lust in our lives. We give God all we are and all we think we are because He wants all. He wants us to hold nothing back.

Only those who seek Him can stand in His Holy Place.

Who shall ascend into the hill of the Lord? or who shall stand in his holy place? He that hath clean hands, and a pure heart; who hath not lifted up his soul unto vanity, nor sworn deceitfully. He shall receive the blessing from the Lord, and righteousness from the God of his salvation. This is the generation of them that seek him, that seek thy face, O Jacob (Psalm 24:3-6).

Only those who really want to see Him face to face will press in to the Holy of Holies by coming to the golden altar. We come of our own volition to let worship flow spontaneously from our heart.

God wants us to come to Him, but He will not force us. He waits patiently for us to come with worship flowing from our hearts through our lips to His heart. We can communicate our hearts to Him and bring our petitions to Him. We can intercede for all our needs and the needs of others. We can take everything to the mercy seat, where we will find "grace to help in time of need" (Hebrews 4:16).

Place of Communion

The golden altar, the mercy seat and the ark of the covenant (or testimony) are so closely connected—like spirit, soul and body—that it is impossible to talk about one without the other. You will see them interwoven throughout the remaining chapters.

As a natural consequence of true worship, we will be ushered into the Most Holy Place to commune with the Father. We can come confidently to this step of intimacy because we have completed the others.

Completing the previous steps toward intimacy in our marriage will usher us into a place of communion with our husbands as well. Once we have accepted them as head, based on our present knowledge and understanding of God's Word, we can open our hearts and share freely with them out of our commitment of love. We can come to our husbands realizing they "paid a price" to have us as their brides. We belong to them in a blood covenant relationship for life. We can come to them with a meek spirit and express appreciation for all they do to bless us. We come not with an attitude of control but one of submission and thanksgiving. We don't come to our husbands with a "look what I've done for you" attitude that will make them feel obligated to spend time with us for all our "good works." Such an attitude will never bring us into true intimacy.

We do not come to our husbands because of our performance. Excitement generated by our sensuality will not bring intimacy in our relationship; it will only turn the focus to us and create lust.

We do not come into intimacy because of an attitude of sacrifice. "I really want to do something else, but I'll sacrifice to be with you." Such an attitude will make a man feel second-rate, unimportant, not valued or revered.

We do not come into intimacy based on past efforts. Each intimate moment with our husbands is new and fresh as we recognize our feelings for each other now that we have taken these steps toward intimacy.

We must come to our husbands with expressions of love and adoration in an attitude of surrender. We should let them know how much we appreciate all they do for us. We should affirm them and express our love spontaneously.

We reverence them by focusing on who they are, not on what they can do for us. They are the love of our lives. We may express joy over them with singing, by dancing with them or by playing an instrument as an expression of our love for them.

Any compliments or appreciation our husbands give to us must not be hoarded in our spirits. We must be grateful and give them to God, not allowing a lascivious or covetous spirit to come into our lives.

The more we daily honor and adore our husbands—in a way they can receive—the more likely they will be to communicate with us on a deep level. Communication of hearts is the foreplay to greater intimacy and causes us to express our love mentally and physically.

Communication from our hearts releases our spirits so we can receive our husbands' provision, protection and love. This prepares us for the mercy seat to enjoy a release of our minds.

Come With Me

Come walk with me.
Come talk with me.
Let us share.
Let us care.
Fellowship.
Make the most of it.
For we are friends!

—*Cheryl Justice*

Chapter Eight

Communion—Atonement

SIXTH STEP OF INTIMACY—MERCY SEAT

The Most Holy Place, sometimes called the Holy of Holies, is where we find the mercy seat resting upon the ark of the covenant. These pieces of furniture represent Jesus, the Life. "Jesus said unto her, I am the resurrection and the life: he that believeth in me, though he were dead, yet shall he live: And whosoever liveth and believeth in me shall never die" (John 11:25-26). There is no life unless there is a resurrection and no need for resurrection if there is no death. We die to ourselves at the mercy seat to come alive in Jesus, represented by the ark of the covenant.

The mercy seat and ark of the covenant appear as one, yet are separate pieces made for each other. Scripture details their differences. The ark is a box—a container to hold Aaron's rod, the pot of manna and the tables of commandments. The mercy seat is an elaborate, movable lid. They are separate for access and for clarity of their respective symbolisms.

In particular, the mercy seat represents the sixth step of intimacy. Made of pure gold (Exodus 25:17), it is located behind the second veil of the tabernacle in the Most Holy Place. "And thou shalt put the mercy seat upon the ark of testimony in the most holy place" (Exodus 26:34).

This piece of furniture correlates with the Feast of Atonement (or Feast of Great Day of Atonement) when a sin offering of atonement was made to God (Numbers 29:7-11). This offering was made once a year by the high priest for the sins of the people. At this time God forgave their sins because they came to Him in obedience.

Here again we find the golden altar, mercy seat and ark of the covenant so closely woven together that it is difficult to talk about one without talking about the other.

At the golden altar our human need for mercy becomes obvious when we focus on who God is. We can now meet with Him face to face as He communes with us.

> And there will I meet with thee, and I will commune with thee above the mercy seat, from between the two cherubims which are upon the ark of the testimony, of all things which I will give thee in commandment unto the children of Israel (Exodus 25:22).

God wants to commune with us. He wants our fellowship. Our obedience in taking each step of intimacy brings us to this place where we can commune with Him. Repentance and forgiveness take place at the mercy seat; that is, repentance on our part and forgiveness on His. Then He can show us the path of His perfect will.

David showed us what kind of attitude brings God's direction for our lives when he said, "Search me, O God, and know my heart: try me, and know my thoughts: and see if there be any wicked way in me, and lead me in the way everlasting" (Psalm 139:23-24). Like David, we can ask God to search our hearts and show us where we are not going God's way. We can be honest like David who realized he was a sheep that needed a shepherd.

Needs in our lives are usually manifested by some sort of problem. Problems are often a result of our negligence to follow God's direction either out of ignorance or disobedience. When we come to the throne of God we become keenly aware of needs in our finances or physical bodies. Emotional or mental problems may get our attention. Jesus can be touched with our weaknesses because He was tempted in everything just as we are (see Hebrews 4:15-16). However, He did not sin. Although He walked in situations similar to ours, He always received the grace of God. Every time He prayed, He opened Himself fully to the Father and received His guidance. Now He has grace and mercy for us in every situation. As we empty all the junk from our lives, we can receive all He has to give us.

All sorts of problems arise when we go our way instead of God's. "There is a way that seemeth right unto a man, but the end thereof are the ways of death" (Proverbs 14:12). This is illustrated by what happened in Fawnia's life.

Fawnia's Story

My daughter Fawnia faced a life-and-death struggle that helped her discover and be set free from some deep needs in her life. When she and her husband, David, were married, they had a three-point plan:

1. Finish their master's programs at CBN University
2. Work to build up their finances so Fawnia could stay home when they started a family
3. Establish their relationship as husband and wife for at least a year before having children.

However, in their fourth month of marriage Fawnia, three months' pregnant, became deathly ill. Unable to keep down any food, she missed too many days from work and was forced to quit. This put a strain on their finances, since both were in graduate school. Because of illness, Fawnia also was behind in her studies but didn't feel she could withdraw from her classes. They were already paid for, and the withdrawal period was over, so there could be no refund.

This created a stressful situation. Because Fawnia quit her job, there was not enough money for David to continue his graduate work beyond that semester. This presented yet another problem. If neither were attending the university, they couldn't remain in student housing. Besides, how could they afford to have this baby?

Perhaps Fawnia's greatest weight was feeling that she wasn't carrying her share of the load. She felt her husband would be disappointed with her. She also felt he would have too great a burden with all the financial responsibility on him.

When I heard how ill Fawnia was, I drove from Tennessee to Virginia. When I first saw her, she hadn't eaten for a week. She was skin and bones, too weak to walk. Even her speech was labored.

Another week passed, and still she could not eat. David and I interceded for her every day. Thursday night we stood beside her bed and began to pray. We learned later that Fawnia wanted to tell us, "Pray until you pray through," but she was too weak to speak. However, God put the urgency in our hearts, and we prayed until we reached a place of peace in our spirits. We "prayed through."

During this prayer, God released Fawnia from the weight of the financial burden and assured her He would restore her. Then she fell asleep.

The next morning Fawnia awakened hungry and able to

eat. She had decided to quit school and not pursue another job. She would stay home, rebuild her health and deliver a healthy baby. She gave all her fears concerning finances and family relationships to the Lord. She received His strength to obey what He had put on her heart to do.

What seemed impossible Thursday worked out Friday! Fawnia and David unexpectedly received a sizable check that more than covered their expenses. Fawnia's adviser at the university agreed to see to her withdrawal from classes and secure a refund. Student Housing allowed them to remain in their apartment until the baby was born. (The day baby Jeremiah was born, they signed papers to buy a house!) God's miraculous timing!

Once Fawnia discovered the need to give her will to God at the mercy seat, He gave her far more than she would have received had she continued going her own way.

Fawnia needed boldness to meet God face to face at the mercy seat in the throne room. Once she faced Him there, she was ready to receive His communion. In His light, her needs and lack of trust were exposed. Now she could quit doing things her way and do them His way. God's way offered much better provision with much less pressure than her way. The surrender of her will made His will possible. His will brought covenant blessings of abundant life.

Problems in our lives often enable us to realize we have been going our own way instead of following the leading of the Spirit. Through God's mercy we are forgiven and able to submit to His leadership.

> Trust in the Lord with all thine heart; and lean not unto thine own understanding. In all thy ways acknowledge him, and he shall direct thy paths. Be not wise in thine own eyes: fear the Lord, and depart

from evil. It shall be health to thy navel, and marrow to thy bones. Honour the Lord with thy substance, and with the firstfruits of all thine increase: so shall thy barns be filled with plenty, and thy presses shall burst out with new wine (Proverbs 3:5-10).

God gives abundantly, fulfilling His covenant with us.

Having therefore, brethren, boldness to enter into the holiest *by the blood of Jesus*, by a new and living way, which he hath consecrated for us, through the veil, that is to say, his flesh; and having an high priest over the house of God; *let us draw near* with a true heart in *full assurance of faith*, having our hearts sprinkled from an evil conscience, and our bodies washed with pure water. Let us hold fast the profession of our faith without wavering: (for he is faithful that promised) (Hebrews 10:19-23, *italics added*).

Faith is necessary to enter His presence and face the Almighty. Trust is necessary to believe that when He shows us our unrighteousness, He does so for fellowship that cannot be experienced without cleansing first. It takes love to draw near to Him, knowing that in the bright light of His presence, we will be further humbled by what we see in our lives.

Can you hear Him say, "Come, My child, sit on My knee; let Me comfort you"? He has invited you to come boldly into His presence. He has known all your sins all the time, yet He still accepts you. He wants you to be confident of His love so you will come into His presence and tell Him all about yourself. He will forgive every sin and allay every fear. He waits for you to come to Him now. What comfort it is to settle everything between us and our Creator! Without the mercy seat, we would only find judgment. ". . . But to this man will I look, even to him that is poor and of a contrite spirit, and trembleth at my word" (Isaiah 66:2).

In 1 John 1:8-9 we are told, "If we say that we have no sin, we deceive ourselves, and the truth is not in us. If we confess our sins, he is faithful and just to forgive us our sins, and to cleanse us from all unrighteousness."

David came honestly and humbly before the Lord in Psalm 86:1-7. He asked God to hear him because he was poor and needy. He confessed his profession of faith. By faith he said he was holy. By faith he declared that God was his God. By faith he asked God to save him. By faith he confessed his trust in God. David cried to God daily and wanted God to be merciful to him. He lifted up his mind to the Lord. He chose to think on God, and he remembered these words: "For thou, Lord, art good, and *ready to forgive;* and *plenteous in mercy* unto *all* them that *call* upon thee" (Psalm 86:5, *italics added*).

Then David pleaded with God to hear his supplication and confessed he would call on the Lord when he was in trouble. He spoke the wonderful truth that God would answer him. Then he worshiped God again by confessing who God is. He was ready to hear from God and receive any instructions God had for him. He continued giving praise: "But thou, O Lord, art a God full of compassion, and gracious, longsuffering, and plenteous in mercy and truth" (Psalm 86:15).

"Justice and judgment are the habitation of thy throne: *mercy* and *truth* shall go before thy face" (Psalm 89:14, *italics added*). While we are before the golden altar in prayer on our way to the Holy of Holies to meet Him face to face, mercy and truth are already there waiting for us. "No good thing will he withhold from them that walk uprightly. . . . Blessed is the man that trusteth in thee" (Psalm 84:11-12). He delights for us to come to the mercy seat to position ourselves to receive all He has to give.

Provision Through Our Husbands

Because we have taken the first six steps of intimacy with God and with our husbands, we are ready to come face to face with our husbands at the mercy seat. We can come in love, compassion and graciousness, ready to forgive as they commune with us. We come with their best interest at heart. By faith we enter into a loving discourse of communion of hearts.

Whether our husbands will admit it, they truly desire intimacy of spirit, soul and body. Sharing with us is much easier for them when they know we are loyal and will not embarrass them over the things they share.

When we listen with our heart to hear from our husbands' heart, they are much more inclined to open up. We can ponder everything they share, whether positive or negative, and be willing to ask forgiveness when necessary.

Just saying we are sorry does not always tear down barriers and set us free. But asking for forgiveness sincerely and waiting for forgiveness from our husbands removes barriers and tears down strongholds, setting us free. They are also freed, and we are bonded together instead of bound up. Because barriers are removed, division leaves, and oneness is restored in those areas discussed.

I've heard some women say, "Well, I've confessed to God, and that's enough. I don't have to confess to my husband." We need to confess our faults to our husbands because doing so gives them the opportunity to forgive us. The Word says they cannot be forgiven by God the Father if they do not forgive us.

For if ye forgive men their trespasses, your heavenly Father will also forgive you: But if ye forgive not men their trespasses, neither will your Father forgive your trespasses (Matthew 6:14-15).

If we confess to God but not to our husbands, we are not really serious about settling everything in our relationship with God. He said in His Word, "Confess your faults one to another . . . that ye may be healed" (James 5:16). Confessing to our husbands specific areas of hurt assures us of the opportunity to be healed of those hurts so no root of bitterness will be able to spring up and defile us (see Hebrews 12:15). We will then be able to pray for others with similar needs and see them healed.

James 5:16 says, "The effectual fervent prayer of a righteous man availeth much." We must be specific and call our sin or fault by name. If it is pride, say pride; if lust, call it lust; if hatred, say hatred. Whatever the sin is, we must be specific to God and man to forever rid our lives of it.

This process is somewhat like the physical body trying to rid itself of poisons. When the blood cell gives up poison into the bloodstream, the blood carries it to the appropriate eliminating organ in the body. If the organ cooperates, the poison will leave the body. If the organ does not cooperate, the poison is reabsorbed into the cells to continue doing its damage. It may show up right away, or it may not show up until later in life.

If we do not cooperate with God's plan by confessing our specific fault or sin to one another, the fault will remain to continue to do its damage.

Matthew 12:34 says, ". . . Out of the abundance of the heart the mouth speaketh." To fully be rid of our faults or sins, we must speak them out of our hearts to the Father in the name of Jesus, asking for His forgiveness. Then we speak out of our hearts more specific things to our husbands, asking their forgiveness.

True oneness cannot be restored until truth and mercy have met together in our lives as husbands and wives. "Mercy and truth are met together; righteousness and peace have kissed each other" (Psalm 85:10). This intimacy of oneness in marriage takes place when we are merciful to each other under the Holy Spirit's direction. God knows when to show us things, past or present, to confront in our lives. We must continually come to the throne room, to the mercy seat, face to face with Him so He can expose any darkness in our lives. We must come face to face with each other in our marriage to expose any barriers or would-be barriers.

The honesty, or *truth*, we give to each other in confession calls for forgiveness, or *mercy*. As we come to our husbands honestly, we acknowledge our need for them. We need their reasoning power, their goal-oriented thinking, to bring direction and protection to our lives. We need their wisdom and their understanding. Our husband is our provider. We can receive provision from him as we empty ourselves of our independence and surrender to him, trusting God to enable him. In a sense, we're at our husband's mercy.

This is a picture of truth and mercy kissing to bring right relationship and unity of mind. Acting on these *right things* (righteousness) will bring *peace of mind* to the marriage.

Our call from God is "Come." So simple, yet often so hard to do. We should come surrendering our independence to Jesus as Lord, yielding to His way to be prepared to do His will. "Come boldly unto the throne of grace . . ." (Hebrews 4:16).

If we need more grace from God to accept the provision He offers us through our husbands, we can find that grace and help we need at the mercy seat. Then we can come to our husbands, hearing from them, looking past their faults to their needs. As we face them with grace for their need for our submission, we can receive whatever they are prepared to provide. As we continue to intercede to the Father for them, they will become more adequate in their provision, and we will continue to grow together in love, acceptance and forgiveness. Our husbands delight for us to come to them in a posture of receiving their provision and protection as we experience a release of hindrances from our minds.

As we draw closer to each other in obedience to God's plan for marriage under the lordship of Christ, we are drawn closer to the Father who brings us to that desired covenant— oneness at the ark of the covenant.

Prayer for Wives to Pray

Father, in Jesus' name, I praise You for giving me such a wonderful husband to be my provider, protector and lover.

I praise You for creating such a beautiful plan for us to enjoy the ultimate in intimacy. I am grateful Your plan is sufficient to cause our needs to be met as man and wife.

Thank You for the wisdom and knowledge of the Word You are bringing to my husband. Thank You that I can trust You to continue enlightening him to Your ways and strengthening him to be an obedient child of God.

Forgive me for every time I have missed an opportunity to pray for my husband.

I ask Your forgiveness for every time I have treated my marriage lightly and have not been the respectful wife I need to be for my husband.

Forgive me for every time I have been selfish and thought of only my needs, my sensitivities, my hurts and my problems. Help me to be more sensitive to his needs and more considerate of my husband's feelings. I pray I will be able to lay down my life for him daily.

Forgive me for every time my expectations of him have been too high, and help me to trust You to meet my needs. Help me to be patient, trusting You to bring forth continual growth in my husband's life.

Forgive me, Father, for every time I have tried to manage my husband or control him. Help me to allow him room to make decisions and to fail, if need be.

I ask Your forgiveness, Father, for every time I have not been totally honest with my husband and shared the truth in love. Help me to be strengthened in You to be wise in my words and to share my heart with him.

Please forgive me for the times I have not surrendered myself in submission to my husband. Help me to lean on You, Father, and not on my own understanding concerning my husband. Help me to receive all he is able to provide in this marriage with a grateful heart.

Help my husband to be guided by Your Holy Spirit daily as He hears Your voice and not the voice of man. May He seek first the kingdom of God and Your righteousness, knowing all the other things he needs will be added to him if he does.

Help him to continue in Your Word daily that his life may be filled with praise, honor and glory to Your name.

Help me to love him with Your love, Father, and learn more of Your ways to bless him. May I support him and be his helpmeet. In Jesus' name, I praise You, Father. Amen.

This prayer is an example of speaking the truth to God about ourselves at the mercy seat. To the extent we surrender to what God already knows about us, we have the mind of Christ, who is the Head of this relationship. Our repentance to God reveals that we are respectfully hoping in His mercy.

"The Lord taketh pleasure in them that fear him, in those that hope in his mercy" (Psalm 147:11). He takes pleasure in those who make themselves vulnerable to Him this way. Hoping in His mercy brings us ever closer to God to enjoy greater fellowship and communion in this restoration of one mind and one accord.

In His light and glory God meets us with amazing grace and plenteous mercy. Darkness is dispelled, and only the shadows of our human needs remain to be exposed by the light in future visits to the mercy seat.

Our husbands take pleasure in our respectful attitude of surrender as we honor them as head by hoping in their mercy. How great God is to recognize our need for companionship with our husbands and with Him!

Loving

Loving is living!
We're never more alive
   Than when we love.
Love turns on lights.
It dispels darkness
   And overcomes evil.
Only shadows remain
   To remind us of our
   Need for love.

—*Cheryl Justice*

Chapter Nine

Communion—Rest

SEVENTH STEP OF INTIMACY—ARK OF COVENANT

Ultimate Intimacy

We have come to the last step of intimacy in the Most Holy Place. The last piece of furniture is the ark of the testimony, or ark of the covenant, upon which sat the mercy seat.

The ark contained the pot of manna, the tablets of the law and Aaron's rod that budded. The ark and its contents symbolize significant truths about Jesus, and I believe they also represent the unity of the Father, Son and Holy Spirit—manna representing Christ, the Bread come down from heaven; the law, the righteousness of God; and the rod, the life of the Holy Spirit.

Jesus declared that He is "the way, the truth and the life: no one cometh unto the Father, but by me" (John 14:6). Today we are tabernacles of righteousness. Christ dwells in us by the person of the Holy Spirit. Thus, we have the Way, the Truth and the Life in our hearts just as the ark contained them symbolically in the Most Holy Place. Through His mercy

143

we have peace and rest in Christ (Psalm 85:10-13).

> Know ye not that ye are the temple of God, and that the Spirit of God dwelleth in you? If any man defile the temple of God, him shall God destroy: for the temple of God is holy, which temple ye are (1 Corinthians 3:16-17).

The ark was a holy place because Jesus dwelled there. If we are the temple of God, we are a holy place where God dwells in the power of the Holy Spirit by Jesus Christ.

The ark also corresponds with the final feast, the Feast of Tabernacles. This feast represented a time of rest after the harvest ended. God commanded the children of Israel to build booths and dwell in them, rejoicing before the Lord for seven days. The harvest was over, the grain collected, and they were thankful. Thus, they celebrated, and they rested.

> Ye shall dwell in booths seven days; all that are Israelites born shall dwell in booths: That your generations may know that I made the children of Israel to dwell in booths, when I brought them out of the land of Egypt: I am the Lord your God (Leviticus 23:42-43).

God said He inhabited the praise of Israel in Psalm 22:3. When Israel filled their booths with praise, rejoicing before the Lord, they found themselves in God's presence.

I believe this is an illustration of New Testament Christians. "For in him dwelleth all the fullness of the Godhead bodily. And ye are complete in him, which is the head of all principality and power" (Colossians 2:9-10).

This oneness with God the Father has come to us in

answer to the prayer Jesus prayed in the garden almost 2,000 years ago. "That they all may be one; as thou, Father, art in me, and I in thee, that they also may be one in us: that the world may believe that thou has sent me" (John 17:21).

He talked about our reaching oneness while we are on earth so the world may believe God sent Jesus. God intends to show Himself to the world through us, the tabernacles of the Holy Spirit. But the world can see Jesus only if He dwells in us and our lives reveal Him. This can be accomplished if we are dead to ourselves and our lives are hid with Christ in God (Colossians 3:3).

What rejoicing we can experience in this blessed fellowship with the Father of all creation! This covenant relationship in which God asks for all we have in exchange for all He has calls for rejoicing! We bring our filthy rags of self-righteousness to receive His robe of righteousness. We bring our sins of destruction to the mercy seat, and He gives us life more abundantly (see John 10:10). Jesus laid down His life so we can have life. Now our attitude should be "my life for yours."

This Christian attitude of "my life for yours" conquers the enemy. Just as Satan couldn't take Jesus' life because He gave it, so he can't take our lives because we give our lives *to* Jesus and *for* Him.

We can sing and dance before the Lord with our hearts filled with praise as we take joy in Him! We can clap our hands and shout aloud with the voice of triumph because Christ is in us! He is the hope of glory! Because Jesus lives in us, Luke's words come alive:

> The Spirit of the Lord is upon me, because he hath anointed me to preach the gospel to the poor; he hath sent me to heal the brokenhearted, to preach deliverance to the captives, and recovering of sight

to the blind, to set at liberty them that are bruised;
to preach the acceptable year of the Lord (Luke
4:18-19).

The Acceptable Year of the Lord

In the Year of Jubilee, a time of great happiness and rejoicing, no blessing was announced by the blowing of the trumpet *until* the Day of Atonement. God said on the Day of Atonement, ". . . Ye [shall] return every man unto his possession" (Deuteronomy 3:20). Health for body and soul is provided in the atonement of Christ. Provision for our internal and external being—the spiritual and the physical—was made in the work of Christ.

God's generous provision was so we can possess the land as Joshua did. The enemy does not want to relinquish our promised possession. Our vile enemy has stolen millions of children from their mothers' wombs. He has used lust and greed to remove millions of husbands from their wives. He has lured teenagers from their homes and onto the streets. He has turned the hearts of fathers away from their children through selfishness. This enemy has brought sickness, disease, despair, sorrow and grief across the land. Through subterfuge, he took prayer and the Bible from our schools. He caused children to be abused by their own godless parents. And he accomplished this through the deception that secular education could do more for us than faith in God.

By the work of Christ we can receive the benefits of the ark of the covenant in the Most Holy Place. We are invited to commune with Him daily. He has enabled us to go forth in the power of His might to confront the enemy and prevail. Jesus has preached the acceptable year of the Lord! Pentecost has come! The spiritual work has been completed to enable us for the task before us.

We are more than conquerors (see Romans 8:37). We can go forth confidently in our nation as into Canaan. Our enemy is already defeated. Our work is to believe on Jesus who was sent by God. He has equipped us "for such a time as this" (Esther 4:14). Jesus is our shield and buckler. He's our rock and our strength. God has already given to us everything that pertains to life and godliness through our Lord Jesus Christ (see 2 Peter 1:3).

He can do His work in this world through us. As we go forward into battle, He fights through us. Christ, the King of Glory, indwells us. Christ the Lord defeated our enemy. We only do what He commands us to do. We only go when He commands us to go. We only speak what He commands us to speak. We go as one with Him. We delight in Him. He delights in us.

Though we are engaged in spiritual warfare, we can rest because the battle is the Lord's. We become channels for Him to accomplish His will in us and through us. Obedience is the key.

We can cease from our own works, from trying so hard. We enter His rest as we continually intercede to the Father through the power of the Holy Spirit. We can rest because we are fully convinced that God loves us with an everlasting love. He is the lover of our souls.

Jesus taught us to pray after this manner: "Our Father which art in heaven, Hallowed be thy name. Thy kingdom come. Thy will be done in earth, as it is in heaven" (Matthew 6:9-10). We come to Him at the *golden altar* when we honor Him as Father and hallow His name. This releases our hearts in a love relationship and allows His Spirit to reign.

His kingdom comes to us as we surrender our wills at the *mercy seat*. This releases our minds for His will to reign.

"Thy will be done on earth as it is in heaven" is coming

to Him at the ark of the covenant to allow the consummation of covenant relationship. This releases bodies so the work of God can come forth.

We experience the ultimate intimacy with God when spirit, soul and body are united in fellowship with Him.

For wives this final step of intimacy is consummated in covenant relationship by the release of our whole self. Covenant relationship grows when love reigns. Surrendering to our husbands results in oneness as we fully accept ourselves as His body. We are ready to experience what oneness means with our husbands under God.

Nevertheless neither is the man without the woman, neither the woman without the man, in the Lord. For as the woman is of the man, even so is the man also by the woman; but all things of God (1 Corinthians 11:11-12).

Neither was the man created for the woman; but the woman for the man (1 Corinthians 11:9).

As we keep in mind that God made us for our husbands, we can enjoy oneness that brings satisfaction to our lives. As a result, we enjoy the "rest" God brings to us because of our obedience. We can cease from taking on responsibilities that are not ours.

We can be free through obedience to God in His call for us to release our hearts fully to our husbands, honoring and appreciating them as the head of our union. Our full acceptance of them helps bring joy and value to their lives. (This was represented by the golden altar.)

We can experience more freedom to surrender our independence to our husbands. This leaves them free to fulfill their God-given responsibilities in the marriage and to experience greater fulfillment as a male. (This was represented by the mercy seat).

Then we are able to surrender our bodies to our husbands to complete them and bear the fruit of their labors. (This is represented by the ark of the covenant.)

We can experience the joy of friendship, partnership and companionship with our husbands if we let the steps of intimacy with God be our pattern for intimacy with our husbands. We can enjoy a beautiful and satisfying time of lovemaking in this *love* relationship as we boldly release our hearts in love expressions, release our minds of independence and release our bodies to receive the ultimate intimacy.

This joyful expression of "laying down our lives" in the intercourse of body, soul and spirit is not only a blessing for us. New life can be conceived at this time, not just in the physical but also in the heart and mind.

Because we have become channels through which our husbands' life can flow, together we can enjoy the fruit of our labor of love. We can be like the Holy Spirit's anointing on our husband's life so he can go forth more than a conqueror.

As we reveal Christ and the Church to the world, we can be like the butterfly and enjoy days of heaven on earth.

Friendship

Friendship . . . most blessed relationship we share.
Physical oneness is only a shadow of the unity
experienced in true friendship . . . that is love
which even lovers seldom know.

—*Cheryl Justice*

Epilogue

'That I May Know Him'

Brenda Taylor had an insatiable desire for intimacy with the Lord. The Word was daily manna to her. She prayed continually. She displayed an eagerness to hear from the Lord and a resolve to promptly do His bidding. The prayer of her heart was to "know him, and the power of his resurrection, and the fellowship of his sufferings, being made conformable unto his death" (Philippians 3:10). That desire became fulfillment June 17, 1996, when she went home to be with the Lord she loved so much.

Heaven now has a greater attraction for those who knew Brenda Taylor. Her life, and even her death, challenged us to a greater resolve in our commitment to follow Christ and to be like Him. The closing pages of this book are a collection of thoughts and feelings about the legacy she left not just to her husband, Al; her children, Fawnia, Todd and Athena; and her grandchildren, Jeremiah, Micah, Bethany, Taylor and Tori;

but to her extended family, to her friends and prayer partners, and to the denomination she loved and served.

Al Taylor

Brenda had a wonderful simplicity about life. God was first. Therefore, she chose to give Him worship every day.

Family was next. As long as I knew her, she wasn't even tempted to enter the workforce to earn more money for the family to have a more affluent lifestyle. She would rather be with her family for an improved spiritual level than to have better things.

As she prayed, she also listened. The Lord would direct her regarding people who needed intercession. Her most typical response to every need was "Let's pray for that need right now." Brenda felt certain the Lord was directing her to give up her wonderful Sunday school class and leave the church we had enjoyed and served for 18 years. Where was He sending her? To Crowder Chapel and its ministry to the poor. When she told the pastor at Crowder of God's instruction to her, he responded that they had been praying for a spiritually mature woman to help with visitation. She was an answer to prayer.

In August 1994 as we departed Cleveland, Tennessee, for our drive to San Antonio, Texas, to attend the Church of God General Assembly, Brenda shared with me that God had just informed her that she would have to give a speech at this assembly. I asked her what He wanted her to speak about, and she declared that God had not told her that part. I reminded her that the program had been finalized a long time ago. She said she knew that, but God would take care of the details.

On Thursday of assembly week, she fasted and prayed all day, seeking God for the message and other particulars. God answered that she would deliver a message of identification repentance for the laity of the church. Further, He instructed that He would tell her when to go into the auditorium to speak.

Friday afternoon God sent her into the General Assembly business session. That particular session was a bit rancorous as proposals to give laymen more ministry opportunities were discussed harshly and rejected. That was the mood when she stepped to the microphone. The general overseer recognized her and asked what she wanted to address. He then instructed her to come to the platform and discuss it with an Executive Committee member. Then, if possible, they would accommodate her request to speak.

Brenda shared with Ray Hughes the content of her message. He responded that he was going to recommend to Lamar Vest, chairman, that she speak. She returned to her seat, and the business session continued. When she decided they had forgotten her, Brother Vest said, "Brenda Taylor asked for permission to make a statement of privilege, and we are going to hear her now."

When she began to speak, the anointing of the Holy Spirit was so heavy upon her until people began to weep throughout the auditorium. By the time she concluded, most people were in tears. Then the men stood up spontaneously and gave her a standing ovation. When the ovation was over, the Holy Spirit spoke through tongues and interpretation. It was a solemn moment in a church desperately in need of a genuine solemn assembly.

Here are the messages: first, the message delivered by Brenda and, second, the transcription of the message given through tongues and interpretation.

Statement of Privilege. To me the things that have been said during this General Assembly are an indication of a need for healing and reconcilement between the laity and the leaders and/or clergy. I see forgiveness as the first step for breaking down barriers. If we are going to cooperate and operate as one and work together to bring the lost and dying world to Jesus Christ, I believe all barriers need to be brought down. The Lord has put on my heart to represent the laity in asking the leaders and clergy for forgiveness in some specific areas for our fathers, forefathers and ourselves. This does not represent everyone, but it will represent someone somewhere at some time. Many of these represent feelings that I have had in my heart at one time or another over the years. I would like to ask this body to forgive me and any of the laymen who have ever had

• Lack of respect for our leaders and clergy
• Attitude of vengeance, such as withholding of tithes, offerings, talents or gifts because we disagree with the way things are done
• For any idolatry for putting you on a pedestal and looking to you as our source instead of to God
• For having higher expectations of you than you could fulfill
• Lack of faith in the almighty God who lives in you and is conforming you to the image of Christ
• For the times that we have quenched the Spirit, not being bold to respond honestly for fear of having all communication cut off between us or being misunderstood
• For the lack of submission; for the many times we have not trusted God to use you as the instruments to help mold our lives
• For every time we have deceived you and other people around us, pretending to be where we are not in our

spiritual walk, trying to please you instead of God
• For envying you for your gifts, your blessings and your abilities; for every time we have coveted and had jealousy—jealous of the attention and credit you have received
• For any resentment we have held against you, especially over any decisions that we feel you have made that affected our lives in an adverse way
• For every time we have spread rumors instead of telling God about the needs and interceding in the Spirit concerning them
• For competing with you instead of completing you by focusing on fulfilling the specific call God has placed on our lives
• For criticism of the things you did and said instead of looking beyond your faults and seeing that you have needs just like the rest of us do and then taking time to intercede for you until your needs are met
• For every time we have been guilty of accusing and judging and condemning you as you carried out your responsibilities so faithfully
• For not extending to you the same love, acceptance and forgiveness that we so desire from you, and for leaning to our own understanding and going our own way instead of God's way

I want to express appreciation to you for being patient with us as laity and for being willing to take the responsibilities that many of us would not be able to carry. I pray that God will bless you and lift you up this very day.

Interpretation. For I tell you today to repent of

bitterness and unforgiveness and see the healing flow of My Holy Spirit as I reconcile the body of believers. As a light in this dark world, give yourselves to one another in love and see the mighty hand of God at work in your midst.

By the 1996 General Assembly, Brenda was with Jesus. Prophecies pertinent to her death and her dying were presented at her funeral (see Appendix).

The butterfly and the Bible, noted often in this book, were the two symbols Brenda most often referred to as pertinent to her life and ministry. God used the butterfly as an object lesson to help release her from the era of legalism in the church as she was growing up. When the graveside service was ended, a pretty butterfly flew past all the flowers and alighted on her coffin for a few moments to the delight of our grandchildren, who exclaimed, "Look! Grandma Brenda's butterfly!"

Upon returning to the house, the grandchildren wanted to go swimming. David and Bruce, our sons-in-law, and Todd took them to the pool. Soon a colorful profusion of several kinds of butterflies surrounded them and even lighted on them. It never happened before. It hasn't happened again. But it was a special comfort to all of us then and now.

Fawnia Taylor Ricks

There was no greater desire in Mom's life than intimacy with her heavenly Father. She longed to be so full of Him that what would proceed from her would be Him—His presence, His wisdom, His love. God's love for people was evident in her. She wasn't afraid to express what God taught her, no matter how "out of the ordinary." She sought to communicate in humility and love. Her sincere desire was to see the body of Christ reach the fullness of what God intends.

Mom perceived her pursuit of God as a lifelong maturing process. Her love for Jesus was unwavering, and her commitment resolute. She wasn't perfect, but she pursued purity in Christ. She wasn't eloquent, but she purposed to proclaim the good news. Hers was not a worldly beauty, but she radiated God's love and was clothed with the unfading beauty of a meek and quiet spirit.

She was faithful to teach us the Word of Truth. Her daily worship instilled in me the importance of dwelling in God's presence. Her commitment of love and loyalty to us, her children, was unshakable. She confronted me when I strayed, praised me for my accomplishments, comforted me through difficulties and prayed for me faithfully. As I grew up, she became my very best friend and confidant. More than a mother of three, she nurtured faith in the hearts of many.

Her example of relationship and godly submission in her own marriage has proven to be a foundation of strength in mine. She taught me to follow the principles God has established, even when unpopular. I am daily reaping the blessings of this godly heritage in my relationship with my husband, David.

During the days following Mom's death in 1996, God comforted me with passages from Isaiah. In a family gathering my cousin Cari Beasley read from Isaiah comforting words God had also given her:

> The righteous perish, and no one ponders it in his heart; devout men are taken away, and no one understands that the righteous are taken away to be spared from evil. Those who walk uprightly enter into peace; they find rest as they lie in death (Isaiah 57:1-2, *NIV*).

Mom has now fully embraced that uninhibited relationship with God for which she yearned.

Like Abraham, she was blessed to be a blessing. She gave us a legacy of faith and self-abandoning trust in God. As the body of Christ, may we all experience increasing intimacy with our heavenly Father as we commune with Him daily.

Todd Taylor

Mom was one of the most sincere, good-hearted people I have ever known. Following her death, some people have observed that she was a great woman. Others said she was a prophetess.

I've spent a great deal of time considering these evaluations. How did these accounts match with my recollections of her? Although she loved the church, I don't ever remember her being accepted in its social circles. If she had been "great," wouldn't she have been sought socially? What about prophecy? Don't people flock to hear prophets? Weren't they highly revered people in Hebrew tradition?

One question led to another, so I decided to settle for what I hear about her in my heart. I remember her as a servant and a survivor.

Mother's mode of operation was that of a servant. Her obedience seemed to take her to humble places to do humble things. In her simple example of a life, she allowed her life to be an exclamation point, punctuating a cause and truth much greater than herself.

True survivors are seekers. They seek that which matters most—life. Reality shapes their priorities. Sensitivity and awareness expose reality to them and make them vulnerable to the pain of their situation. If survivors are not aware of their need, they will not see the danger of their predicament. They will not seek a solution, and they will not survive. It is this awareness and hopeful tenacity to find a true solution that defines them.

Mom grew up in a church and a culture that sought to achieve holiness through performance—the legalism paradigm. Mom was spiritually needy. She was aware of her need. With tenacity and veracity, she went after what she and so many others had been taught was true. Her need drove her into such an immersion in the counterfeit that she became sick of it; yet her need prevailed and increased. Spiritually sick, physically weak, in desperate need, she sought for something real.

To the hungry, a store will not suffice. No more counterfeits or mirages for Mom. She had crashed too hard too often. As a true survivor she persistently and fervently sought for that which mattered most. She yearned for relationship. She panted for intimacy with Christ. God began revealing things to her. He gently led her, guided her and changed her. She no longer fretted as she had over perfection. As her relationship grew, her freedom grew. The more intimacy with Christ she experienced, the more she wanted.

Preceding her last year on earth, a prayer began forming in her spirit from the Scriptures:

> But what things were gain to me, those I counted loss for Christ. Yea doubtless, and I count all things but loss for the excellency of Christ Jesus my Lord: for whom I have suffered the loss of all things, and do count them but dung, that I may win Christ, and be found in him, not having mine own righteousness, which is of the law, but that which is through the faith of Christ, the righteousness which is of God by faith: That I may know him, and the power of his resurrection, and the fellowship of his

sufferings, being made conformable unto his death (Philippians 3:7-10).

She didn't understand why it was her prayer. She was, however, continually drawn to it.

It's hard to watch anyone die, especially someone you love. In her case it was paradoxical. She was a survivor. Everyone dies. Strangely, as she deteriorated and was in torturous pain, she told us that all the pain was worth it. She felt the intimacy and the warmth of Christ's loving presence.

Mom was a survivor and a servant. As a survivor she sought for the pathway to truth, intimacy with Christ. As a servant she bowed to the greater cause and pointed to The Way.

Athena Taylor Jarman

I am very proud of my mother and the life she lived. She was a godly lady and a prayer warrior. As I was growing up, I always heard her praying in the mornings, interceding for our family and the body of Christ. I know the many prayers she prayed are still effective and are still being answered.

In this book many things are revealed about past problems in our family, as well as some insecurities Mom was still dealing with. Her reason for sharing these things was to encourage those of you who might be facing similar situations and to show how magnificently God can transform us as we follow His beloved Truth, the Word of God. I feel the content of this book is powerful and definitely needed for today's women and their families.

Mom was passionate for Christ, and her life exemplified that beautifully through her relationships with us, her family and the many lives she touched. She was not perfect, of course, but her desire was to know Christ and Him crucified and to truly understand all that encompassed. I'm sure she knows very well now.

Mom, I'm so thankful God allowed you to be in my life, especially as my mother. You were and still are a blessing from the Father. Your love, free spirit and desire for relationship with Christ and your family are an invaluable gift. I will always love you.

The Message of Brenda Taylor's Life

[June 20, 1996—A prophetic message spoken through Dr. Rickie Moore at Brenda Taylor's funeral]

This is a solemn assembly. It is God's solemn assembly. He called us here in His time.

Holy Spirit, we pray that You would give us the strength to do what You are asking each of us to do; in Jesus' name we pray. Amen.

God is the only one who can make an assembly solemn, and He makes it solemn. He shows us how serious He is by what He is willing to sacrifice; He is willing to sacrifice the very best.

Brenda Taylor's life. . . . I have been asked to speak to that. It is an honor beyond words. It is a burden beyond words. I have not been a lifelong friend of Brenda Taylor; there is so much about her life I do not know. I really did not get to know her closely until she was dying; but you know, in her dying, her life was revealed.

The Lord spoke to me one Monday morning after Max Morris preached a sermon the day before at Westmore where he challenged our hearts to listen to the "still, small voice." The next morning that still, small voice told me to go talk to

Brenda Taylor. It was in February [1996], I believe. It was difficult to take that first step to go. I had heard about her cancer and her condition, and to be honest, I felt like there were so many other people that stood between me and her. I did not feel worthy to go. I suppose I felt afraid to go because I did not know what I could say. The Lord told me to go, and so I went.

She met me at her door and invited me into her living room. I was able simply to tell her, "The Lord spoke to me and asked me to come and talk to you, and I don't know what to say." But as I told her about the sermon on that Sunday at Westmore, and as I told her about how the Lord had spoken to me, it occurred to me that there was one question that had cropped up during the weeks that I had heard her name called for prayer at various places all over the city. I remembered how she had taken a step at the denomination's last General Assembly almost two years ago—a step that may in fact even mark the beginning of our solemn assembly, although we may not have recognized it as such. She offered a confession, a confession representative of the body as well as personal, for sins of the laity against the clergy.

I remembered that I had heard something in the months that followed, something that led me to believe that as Brenda Taylor was taking this journey with the Lord into this experience of cancer, listening to the Lord, trying with all of her heart to do only those things she felt the Lord was leading her to do and consequently not availing herself of many medical steps that human wisdom might tell us to take in such a situation, while there were many voices around her as she was striving to listen to that still, small voice in the midst of all of that cacophony of opinions and councils, according to what I had heard, she was understanding her own affliction as something the Lord was asking her to bear in a certain way and to do it to represent a much larger affliction.

So I asked her the question, "Brenda, do you feel this affliction in your body is revealing something about the affliction in the body of the Church?" She smiled. There was no harshness, and matter-of-factly she simply began to say, "Well, yes, I do believe the Lord has spoken to me." And she proceeded to tell me something that made my ears tingle. She said, "I believe the Lord has said to me that the affliction of the body is located in that part of the body that nurtures the children."

The Lord had already prepared me to hear those words. That is another story for another time, but I knew when she spoke those words that this was a word from the Lord. . . . That evening I had supper with my wife, just the two of us, and I told her about my visit with Brenda. I told her that there at Brenda's home I found nothing that felt like death, but rather I encountered an experience that felt like life. I felt like Brenda was telling me all kinds of things about life that I did not know. She was alive! But then I recalled to my wife those words she spoke about the affliction of the body being located in that part of the body that nurtures the children. My wife too had been prepared from things she had heard before, and she knew this was a word from the Lord. So in that moment she said to me, "You may have to do something about that. You may have to share that with someone." And that statement, I believed, was another word from the Lord.

In the days that followed, a tremendous struggle went on inside me as the seed of that word Brenda had told me began to grow into a message I knew was forming inside my soul. Finally, on March 14, a Thursday afternoon in my office, the Lord enabled me to deliver that message. And this is what it said:

The Lord says, "You called a solemn assembly to hear from heaven. Heaven spoke, but you did not hear it. It was not a pretty word; it was a hard word. But you prefer your smooth words, which are lies, to God's hard word, which is true. The word to the Body can be found in the body of Brenda Taylor. Her affliction is an affliction unto death. It is an affliction that is centered in that part of the body that nurtures the children. You say, 'The Church is healthy. It's moving. It's growing.' But I say the malignancy is growing. The malignancy is growing, and the children are starving, but I will not let them starve. They will live, but you will die. I am already sharpening my ax. Its blade is very sharp. Its head is very heavy. It will cut down your systems, your strategies, your schedules and your salaries along with every one who holds on to any of these with as much as one little finger. Your solemn assembly is over; now I am calling Mine. Come and meet Me around the dying body of Brenda Taylor. Come and meet Me there. Do not delay. And do not leave before you have heard from Me. Or else I will come and meet you, and My ax will be in My hand."

That was March 14 of this year [1996]. The message had to wait. One of the reasons it was postponed is that Brenda herself, when it was later shared with her, had some reservations. She had too much love in her heart to be comfortable with a message so hard. God could entrust His message of judgment to the body of Brenda Taylor because she had no judgmental agenda of her own. Her agenda was to give her life, to give up her life, not to fight for it as we are prone to do, as we are doing this very day . . . fighting for our lives . . . scrapping for our lives . . . pushing for our lives . . . dressing for our lives.

God asked Brenda to give her life, and she gave it. But He is not asking any less of any of us.

I called home later in the morning the day I heard of Brenda's death. My little Hannah answered the phone. She said, "Daddy, I heard about Brenda Taylor. Does this mean the church is going to die?"

I had to answer her truthfully. "Yes, it is going to die."

The denomination is dead.

But I said, "You know, Honey, when a sinner hears the Word of the Lord and feels the conviction of the Holy Spirit and steps out of that seat and walks down that long aisle and comes to that altar, that sinner dies! That sinner dies to the life he was leading, to the image he was projecting. It is a death, Honey, but Brenda would want me to tell you, 'It's life.' "

That is her life today. That is the message of her life today. *That is the message of Brenda's life!* She wants us to know, O Church of the Living God, that there is life on the other side of that death, and there is life nowhere else.